Old Testament

Exploring God's Word

Study Guide

By John Scharlemann

CPH
Concordia Publishing House

Edited by Thomas J. Doyle

Write to the Library for the Blind, 1333 S. Kirkwood Road, St. Louis, MO 63122-7295 to obtain this study in braille or large print for the visually impaired.

Scripture taken from the HOLY BIBLE: NEW INTERNATIONAL VERSION®. NIV ® Copyright 1973, 1978, 1984 by International Bible Society. Used by permission of Zondervan Publishing House. All rights reserved.

1   2   3   4   5   6   7   8   9   10   06   05   04   03   02   01   00   99   98   97

Contents

Introduction

The study of the Old Testament is nothing less than an exploration into the thoughts and desires of God for ordinary people like you and me. It takes us from this hardened and selfish world into the promise of a world where God's peace, justice, and mercy will be complete.

Delving into the Bible for the first time can be somewhat intimidating. We are taken to a distant past that is full of unfamiliar customs and traditions. We must become acquainted with a nation that viewed the world differently than many people do today. And we must begin to alter some of our current definitions to grasp the full meaning of our Lord's love and compassion.

As foreign as many customs and traditions might seem to us today, we will discover that people's natures remain the same. We are trapped today—as people were centuries ago—in an imperfect world where evil and pain seem all too prevalent. We, too, can view the world as meaningless and without hope. But Jesus Christ came to rescue the world from its quagmire, and His deliverance continues to change our lives. Pray that the Word of God, as it comes, will begin to alter your perspective. May His promises give you rich and lasting hope and joy!

How to Use This Study

The Study Guide will direct your study of the Old Testament. The typical lesson is divided into five parts:

1. Approaching This Study
2. An Overview
3. Working with the Text
4. Applying the Message
5. Taking the Message Home

"Approaching This Study" is intended to whet the reader's appetite for the topics at hand. It leads participants into the world of the Old Testament while summarizing the issues to be examined. The "Overview" summarizes the textual material used in each lesson. Before the text is examined in detail, it is viewed as a whole, allowing participants to "see the forest" before "exploring the trees." "Working with the Text" draws participants into deeper biblical study, encouraging them to discover the gems of universal truth that lie in the details of God's Word. When questions appear difficult or unclear, the Leader's Guide provides a doorway to the answers. "Applying the Message" leads participants from the recorded Word of God to its possible application in our present lives. It helps participants more fully realize the implications of God's Word for the daily experience of a Christian. Finally, "Taking the Message Home" invites participants to continue their scriptural meditation at home. Suggestions are given for personal reflection, for preview of the following lesson, and for private study of topics raised by the lesson. The study of God's Word will be greatly enhanced by those actively pursuing the suggestions offered in this section.

Each lesson includes some "trivia" that is intended to spark interest and generate additional discussion. This can be used to develop inquisitiveness and enthusiasm about related issues ripe for exploration.

A glossary is provided at the end of this Bible Study. Because a study of the Old Testament will lead participants to language that may occasionally seem foreign and difficult, the glossary will make participants more comfortable with terms, phrases, and customs in the Christian church. It will help them understand biblical concepts such as *covenant, Israel,* and *redeemer* that may differ from current definitions.

The Bible study also incorporates easy-to-read charts and maps that will aid participants in their understanding of biblical geography and chronology. These should be referred to frequently as they give visual support to the context of the lesson.

Session 1

Promises from the Old Testament

Genesis 3:14–15; 12:1–3; Exodus 19:3–6; 2 Samuel 7:4–17

Approaching This Study

The Bible is composed of two divisions of books. The Old Testament books describe God's creation and protection of a chosen people. God selected these people to act as His witnesses to the world. God made certain promises to His people designed to establish them as His chosen ones. These promises point to the coming of a Savior and Messiah. The Old Testament encompasses a period of time from the creation of the world until about 400 years before the coming of Jesus Christ. The New Testament books, on the other hand, begin with the birth of Jesus Christ. They describe His ministry, death, and resurrection as well as the creation of God's church, founded on the Gospel of Jesus Christ and formulated on the teachings of Jesus' apostles. The New Testament encompasses a period of only about 100 years.

Both Testaments are God's inspired Word to us. Everything we read in the Bible is completely reliable and has been recorded for the purpose of leading its readers to salvation in Jesus Christ. The study of the Old Testament provides important preparation for our understanding of Jesus' ministry. The Old Testament describes God's people, Israel, struggling with their faith over many centuries. Throughout its history Israel displayed periods of belief and unbelief. The history of Israel is a spiritual roller coaster. As such, it exemplifies people's utter hopelessness in redeeming themselves, and their total reliance on a Savior who comes from heaven, from the "outside," to redeem the world from sin.

The Old Testament introduces us to God's "Law" and reveals through centuries of human failure our inability to follow that Law perfectly. Israel's repeated mistakes stand in stark contrast to God's holiness and perfection. The history of Israel mirrors each individual's walk with the Lord in this sinful world. The life of faith is not constant. It has its ups

7

and downs. Faith endures periods of strength and weakness, and yet, faith remains God's gift and tool of salvation.

An Overview

Divide the class into four groups. Each group should read and discuss one of the following: Genesis 3:14–15; Genesis 12:1–3; Exodus 19:3–6; and 2 Samuel 7:4–17. Then summarize each promise for the class.

The Message in Brief

These Bible passages each underscore one of the important promises given by God to His people in the Old Testament. By way of these promises, God would introduce His plan for eternal salvation to the entire world. God had chosen the Hebrew nation to bring His message of deliverance to a sin-soaked world. In a pagan, idolatrous world, God established through Israel the knowledge of the one true God. God then promised He would reign as Savior and King forever through King David's line. And although God would ultimately destroy the power of the devil, He would allow His only Son Jesus to endure much suffering in the process.

Working with the Text

The First Messianic Promise (Genesis 3:14–15)

1. In founding the nation of Israel, God created, in a world of idolatry, a people who bore witness to the one, true, living God as our Savior. Israel was part of His plan to bring Christ into the world as our Savior from sin. We read about that "savior" for the first time in Genesis 3:14–15. What had just happened (Genesis 3:1–7)? From what consequence of sin did Adam and Eve need deliverance?

2. According to Luke 3:23–37 (specifically verse 37!), who was Jesus' original human ancestor? How does that make Him "the woman's (Eve's) offspring?" What would happen between the woman's offspring and the serpent? Who would have its head crushed? Who would have

His heel bruised? How does this foreshadow (point to) the death and resurrection of Jesus Christ?

God Chooses His People (Genesis 12:1–3)

1. The Hebrews viewed Abraham as their founding father. Why was that? What action would follow from the promise given by God to Abraham in verse 1? How old was Abraham when he heard and followed God's command (verse 4)?

2. Look up John 8:31–38. Even in Jesus' day, the Jews clung to their chosen status. What blessing did they believe their ancestry provided? Do you think their claim was accurate?

3. Scan the genealogy recorded in Matthew 1:2–16. Specifically, whose name begins the genealogy? And whose name is at the end? Why do you think this is important?

4. Since the coming of Christ, who should be considered part of God's chosen, that is, the "spiritual descendants of Abraham"? As you consider this question, read Galatians 3:6–9 and Romans 4:16–17.

The Role of God's Chosen People (Exodus 19:3–6)

1. God spoke these words through Moses after His people had been rescued from Egyptian slavery and brought to Mount Sinai. How do these verses describe Israel's deliverance? What does God promise Israel if they follow His will? In what way will Old Testament Israel stand as a unique nation?

2. Did God's people live up to their promise? Explain the role of the prophets. (See Jeremiah 3:22–25; Ezekiel 15; Hosea 5:5–7).

3. Describe the events that seemed to indicate the end of God's promise according to 2 Kings 25:1–22.

4. Although God's people no longer enjoyed sovereignty in the Promised Land after these terrible events, had God abandoned them? What does Jeremiah 31:31–34 suggest? How about Isaiah 62:1–5?

A Savior through David's Line (2 Samuel 7:4–17)

1. King David was so thankful for his many blessings that he wanted to build the Lord a permanent place of worship. In the past, God's people had worshiped the Lord in a temporary shelter called the tabernacle. David wanted to build a permanent temple. But who would give

a "house" to whom? How long would this "house" endure? Who ultimately emerged from this "house" according to Luke 2:4–7?

2. How are believers in Christ part of this "house" (1 Peter 2:4–10)? After reading these verses from Peter, describe how Christian ministry resembles that for which Israel was chosen in Exodus 19:3–6?

Applying the Message

1. In a special act of creation, God made Adam and Eve. He chose them to reflect His image of goodness and holiness. But they disobeyed the Lord and were exiled from Eden. One of their descendants was Abraham. God chose Abraham's descendants to be His chosen people, set apart from the world for the purpose of witnessing God's goodness and mercy. In His greatest act of love for His people, God sent His Son, Jesus, to atone for the whole world's sin. Now all people are called through the Gospel to be God's chosen people (although some will reject that call). What does this demonstrate about God's mercy and grace throughout history? How does that influence your perception of God's nature?

2. Share with one another what it means in your life to be "God's chosen" in Jesus Christ. Do you feel worthy of that choice? Why or why not?

3. As we witness "the promises of God" fulfilled in Jesus Christ, what assurance do we have for the present and future?

Taking the Message Home

Review

Reflect on the great promises of the Old Testament. Read again Genesis 3:14–15; Genesis 12:1–3; Exodus 19:3–6; and 2 Samuel 7:4–17. What are the comforting implications of realizing that God always fulfills His promises?

Looking Ahead

Read Genesis 3 before the next session. Why is this the saddest chapter in the Bible? Consider the reasons Adam and Eve broke God's Law. What do you think motivated them? What happened to their faith in God's promises? What were the consequences of their sins?

Working Ahead

Choose one or more of the following suggestions for individual work:

1. Consider the power of the human word. Our words can affect ourselves and others. In what way can words destroy the lives of others? How can they uplift others? How can the words we think to ourselves affect our outlook on the world? Are words essential for human activity? Could we manage without the ability to communicate? If human words can have such impact, imagine the power of God's Word, which created everything out of nothing!

2. Through the inspiration of the Holy Spirit, Moses records a description of the creation of the world and relates accounts that are integral to the formation of God's people in the book of Genesis. What stories from your parents or grandparents have been handed down to you? If you wish, be prepared to share some of these stories at the next session.

3. Although Genesis records accounts about many of God's faithful people, the people are always portrayed with their faults as well as their strengths.

a. What was Adam's fault (Genesis 3:8–12)?

b. How about Noah's (Genesis 9:20–23)?

c. Did Abraham have a weakness (Genesis 16:1–4)?

d. What was Jacob's flaw (Genesis 27:1–36)?

e. How about Judah's (Genesis 38:12–18)?

Why do you think it's important that God's Old Testament people be considered with all of their faults as well as their strengths? How does this lend comfort when we fall short? What does this suggest about the possibility of living a perfect, God-pleasing life? Be prepared to talk about the weaknesses of these biblical heroes at the next session.

Did you know that the Old Testament is composed of 39 books? Seventeen of them record the history of God's people from the time of creation until the return of Israel from Babylon; 17 are written by men who were inspired to declare the prophecies of God; 5 are called "poetic" in that they record in verse the working of God in and among IIis people and the nations of the world.

The Old Testament at a Glance

Reference	Event	Timing
Genesis 1–2	Creation of the World	
Genesis 3	The Fall into Sin	
Genesis 6–9	The Flood	At Least 1,600 Years after Creation
Genesis 11–35	Abraham, Isaac, Jacob	About 450 Years after the Flood
Genesis 37–50	The Story of Joseph	About 400 Years after Abraham
Exodus 1–2	Moses' Birth, Early Life	
Exodus 3–18	Moses Leads Israel from Egypt	
Exodus 20, 32	Giving of the Law; the Golden Calf	
Exodus 33–34; Numbers 12–14; 16, 17, 20–24	Israel's Wanderings in the Wilderness	
Deuteronomy 34	Death of Moses	
Joshua 1–11, 24	Conquering the Land of Canaan	
Judges 1–21; Ruth; 1 Samuel 1–8	The Time of the Judges	Begins 100 Years after Moses
1 Samuel 9–31; 2 Samuel 1–22; 1 Kings 1–5, 8-11	The Kingdom under Saul, David, Solomon	
1 Kings 12–13; 2 Chronicles 10	The Kingdom Splits	
1 Kings 14–22; 2 Kings 1–14; 1 Chronicles 13–27	The Years of Two Kingdoms, Judah and Israel	
2 Kings 15–17	The People of Israel Carried into Captivity	250 Years after the Split in the Kingdom
2 Kings 16; 18–25; 2 Chronicles 28–36; Isaiah 1, 26–39; Jeremiah 1, 19, 21, 26, 36–39, 52	The Kingdom of Judah Continues until the People are Carried into Captivity	140 Years after Israel Carried into Captivity
Daniel 1–6; Esther 1–10; Jeremiah 40–43	The People of Judah in Babylon	A Total of 70 Years
Ezra 1, 3–6; Nehemiah 1,2, 4, 6	The Return from Babylon and Rebuilding of Jerusalem	535 to 445 years before Christ

(From *When God Speaks* by Jack K. Muhlenbruch. Copyright © Concordia Publishing House 1962. All rights reserved.)

Session 2

Genesis: How It All Began

Genesis 1:1–5; 2:8–9, 15–25; 3; 13:14–17; 27:1–29; 35:22–26

Approaching This Study

Scientists are absorbed with curiosity about the beginnings of the universe and the formation of our planet. We have fields of study in which ancient bones, rocks, and fossils are analyzed. It is only natural for us to wonder where our world came from and why we are here. Some people even ask deeper questions, such as, why did Jesus have to die on the cross? Why does God let people sin?

One way to find answers to such questions is to go back to Genesis, the book of beginnings, which is the first book of the Bible. You probably know that Genesis describes the creation of the world, the first plants and animals, and the first man and woman. But you might not be so familiar with its many other accounts. Some involve the first sin and the first murder. Others show how men and women who trusted in God's promises became part of His chosen people. Most important, Genesis demonstrates how God rescued His people when they were in trouble, pointing to the ultimate rescue God would provide all people in the life and work of His Son, Jesus Christ.

Through the narratives in Genesis we get an idea of how people are affected by God's promises. When they refuse to listen, they can expect judgment. But when they believe in His promises, they are blessed in many ways. God's promises encourage His people even when their situation seems hopeless.

In this session we will look at four particular episodes in our "book of narratives." Through these narratives we gain an understanding of our origin and the emergence of sin. We also witness God's election of Abraham as the father of His people, recognizing that the promises given Abraham are passed down to his descendant, Jacob (Israel), who sires 12 sons. Each of these 12 sons is the founding father of one of the "12 tribes of Israel" whose history we follow throughout the Old Testament.

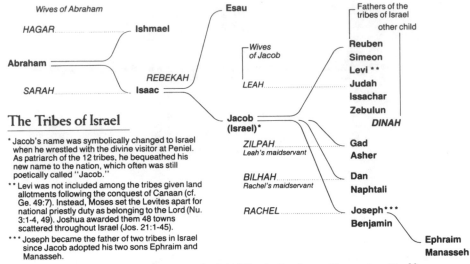

The Tribes of Israel

* Jacob's name was symbolically changed to Israel when he wrestled with the divine visitor at Peniel. As patriarch of the 12 tribes, he bequeathed his new name to the nation, which often was still poetically called "Jacob."

** Levi was not included among the tribes given land allotments following the conquest of Canaan (cf. Ge. 49:7). Instead, Moses set the Levites apart for national priestly duty as belonging to the Lord (Nu. 3:1-4, 49). Joshua awarded them 48 towns scattered throughout Israel (Jos. 21:1-45).

*** Joseph became the father of two tribes in Israel since Jacob adopted his two sons Ephraim and Manasseh.

Taken from the NIV STUDY BIBLE. Copyright © 1985 by the Zondervan Corporation. Used by permission of Zondervan Publishing House.

An Overview

Read Genesis 1:1–5. Describe the "nothingness" that existed before creation. Then read aloud Genesis 2:8–9 and 15–25. Choose five volunteers. Have one read the narrative section of Genesis 3, another the voice of God, a third the voice of Adam, a fourth the voice of Eve, and the last volunteer the voice of the serpent. Read with expression! Then read aloud Genesis 13:14–17; 27:1–29; and 35:22–26.

The Message in Brief

The various readings in this session build the foundation for an understanding of the Old Testament. We learn about God's creative activity in forming the world and the first people. We gain an understanding of the origin of sin and its consequences. We also gain an appreciation of God's mercy and undeserved love in choosing a special people through Abraham and Jacob. These people He will not only bless, but use as a blessing for the rest of the world through the Savior, who would one day be born into their family line.

Working with the Text

A Creation! (Genesis 1:1–5; 2:8–9, 15–25)

1. Who is around at "the beginning"? Before answering this question, be aware that the Hebrew word for *God* ("elohim") is plural. But

the verb for *created* is singular! It would be like saying, "In the beginning *Gods creates* the heavens and the earth." Consider that "God" is not only present at the beginning, but so is the "Spirit of God." And there's even more! Look up John 1:1–5. The "Word," as used by John, is another name for Jesus Christ. If the "Word" is Jesus Christ, then who is also present when God speaks and everything comes into existence?

2. So at the beginning we see God—the Father, the Son, and the Holy Spirit—involved in creation. Does this mean there are three Gods? Look up Deuteronomy 6:4 and Isaiah 44:6 and see what it says.

3. In what activity is the Spirit of God engaged before the creation according to Genesis 1:2? In the New Testament, we see the Spirit descend on Jesus in the form of a dove (Mark 1:10). How is this image of the Spirit consistent with that depicted at creation?

4. After reading Genesis 2:8–9 and 15–25, describe the environment in Eden. What two trees grew in the middle of the garden according to 2:9? Which of these two did God forbid Adam and Eve to eat of? Why did God create Eve?

The Fall (Genesis 3)

1. What animal form does "temptation" take? Who is the serpent according to Revelation 12:9?

2. Focus on Genesis 3:1–5 and the manner in which the serpent tempts Eve. How would you describe his tactics in convincing Eve to disobey the Lord's command?

3. After Adam and Eve fell from the Lord's favor, how did they feel about themselves? Did they go searching for the Lord? Why were they afraid?

4. Describe the strategy Adam and Eve used to shift blame for their sin from themselves.

The Promise to Abraham (Genesis 13:14–17)

1. When Abraham and his nephew, Lot, disputed about their respective use of the land, God led Abraham to his "Promised Land." At the time Abraham was childless. But what promise does God give Abraham about the Promised Land and the descendants who would inhabit it?

2. Now look up Genesis 17:1–10 and explain how God reiterates this promise. Notice how God describes this agreement as a "covenant." This covenant becomes the basis of God's relationship to Abraham's descendants, the people of Israel. Explain what kind of response this covenant required from Abraham's people.

The Blessing Given Jacob (Genesis 27:1–29; 35:22–26)

1. Abraham gave birth to Isaac who in turn gave birth to Jacob and Esau. According to custom, the oldest son would receive a special blessing from his father. Who deserved this blessing? Describe how Jacob—with the help of his mother Rebekah—gained Esau's blessing through deception and fraud.

2. Describe in your own words the blessing Isaac gave Jacob.

3. Jacob's name would be changed by God to "Israel." That name will be used throughout the Old Testament to describe all of Jacob's descendants. Each of Israel's 12 sons would be the ancestor of a unique "tribe" within Israel. The people of Israel, then, would be composed of 12 tribes. Knowing this, why do you think it is significant that Jesus chose 12 disciples to follow Him?

Applying the Message

1. When we ask the question, "Where did the world come from?" the Bible says, "From God—in six days." When we question the origin of sin and evil, the Bible tells us, "From the devil." Why do you think the Bible feels it's unnecessary to go into greater detail about either answers? How does John 20:31 help answer this question? Would you have appreciated more detail? Why or why not?

2. Why do you think Eve wanted to disobey God and eat the forbidden fruit? In what way was her motivation similar to that which lies behind all sin? Adam and Eve ate "from the tree of the knowledge of good and evil." Notice it's not called an apple tree. Do you remember the name of the other tree which grew in the middle of the garden? Remembering the nature of this other tree, how was it a blessing that Adam and Eve were exiled from Eden before they had a chance to eat from it? How does this change your perspective of God's motivation for banishing the two humans?

3. What's your impression of Jacob as he usurped his brother's birthright? Would you trust him as a friend? The name *Jacob* means "supplanter." Why is this appropriate? What is your reaction to the fact that Jacob, despite his unethical ways, was chosen by God to be a father of God's people? How might this give comfort to ordinary, sinful Christians like you and me? Read Romans 5:6–11.

Taking the Message Home

Review

The book of Genesis is crammed full of many narratives. We can't focus on all of them during one lesson. It would be helpful for you to read the entire book, enjoying the many accounts of people who either follow God's guidance or disobey His will. In particular, focus on Cain and Abel (Genesis 4:1–16), the Flood (Genesis 6–9), the Tower of Babel (Genesis 11:1–9), Hagar and Ishmael (Genesis 16), Sodom and Gomorrah (Genesis 19:1–29), the testing of Abraham (Genesis 22), Jacob's dream at Bethel (Genesis 28:10–22), Jacob wrestling with God (Genesis 32:22–32), and the story of Jacob's son, Joseph (Genesis 37; 39–47).

Looking Ahead

Before meeting again for the next session, read Exodus 3 and Deuteronomy 34. The books from Exodus to Deuteronomy relate how God rescued the people of Israel from Egyptian captivity and led them back to their Promised Land. God called a man named Moses to act as their leader. After reading Exodus 3, reflect on Moses' personality. How would you describe his fears and weaknesses?

Working Ahead

Choose one or more of the following suggestions before meeting for the next session:

1. Rent the movie *The Ten Commandments,* starring Charlton Heston. Perhaps you can purchase the video from a catalog. Or maybe you've seen it recently on TV. After viewing it, write down your impression of the movie, particularly the role of Moses. How were the Egyptians depicted? What about the people of Israel?

2. Read the Ten Commandments as recorded in Exodus 20:1–17. Do you think these commandments are as important today as they were in Moses' day? Why or why not?

3. In our next session we will consider Exodus, Leviticus, Numbers, and Deuteronomy. Each of these books are named, appropriately, for their content. Consider, for example, Exodus. Look up the word in a dictionary. Why would this be an appropriate title to describe Israel's flight from Egypt under Moses' leadership? The priests of Israel were to be called from the tribe of Levi. So they were often called Levites. What do you think the book of Leviticus will focus on? In the beginning of Numbers, Moses takes a census of the people. So why is the title *Numbers* appropriate? *Deuteronomy* means "repetition of the Law." What might you expect to find when reading this book?

Did you know that Abraham's wife, Sarah, was also his half-sister? When the Lord announced to Abraham that he would have a son, Sarah was 90 years old, well past child-bearing age. The announcement was later repeated by three strangers, angels in disguise, who visited Abraham and Sarah. When Sarah heard their announcement, she laughed scornfully. It seemed impossible! But in due time the child was born and named Isaac, which in Hebrew means "he laughed!"

Session 3

On to the Promised Land!

Exodus 3; 19:1–20:20; Numbers 13:17–14:25; Deuteronomy 34

Approaching This Study

It is not unusual for people to attempt reading the Bible from cover to cover. With all the best intentions, an individual starts reading Genesis and concludes it's a pretty interesting book. Even the beginning of Exodus is an attention grabber. But then the reader confronts a seemingly endless array of laws recorded in the latter portion of Exodus as well as the three books that follow. Soon the Bible reader may feel frustrated and lost.

We certainly don't want that to happen! It's important to read the rest of God's Word because He has some important messages for us. So as we contemplate Exodus, Leviticus, Numbers, and Deuteronomy, we will examine four highlights. These will give us an overall view of the events from Moses' call as leader of Israel to the moment when God's people are prepared to enter the Promised Land.

Between the time of Jacob's (Israel's) death and the call of Moses, many years elapsed. Jacob's descendants grew in number. Soon they consisted of several million people. They lived in Egypt, and as they rapidly multiplied, the leaders of Egypt became threatened. They decided the people of Israel should become their slaves.

But they were still God's special people. And one day God called Moses to lead His people from their slavery in Egypt to Canaan (Palestine), which was often called "the Promised Land" because this was the land promised many years earlier to Abraham, Isaac, Jacob, and their descendants.

The Lord through Moses demonstrated His resolute will through 10 different plagues against the people of Egypt. After each plague, the king of Egypt first promised to let Israel go, but then reneged. Only after the last and most violent plague (in which all the firstborn males of each Egyptian family died) did Pharaoh finally relinquish his control over Israel. Moses led God's people out of Egypt and into a new world.

But God's people soon forgot He had chosen them. They complained

The Exodus

The exodus and conquest narratives form the classic historical and spiritual drama of OT times. Subsequent ages looked back to this period as one of obedient and victorious living under divine guidance. Close examination of the environment and circumstances also reveals the strenuous exertions, human sin and bloody conflicts of the era.

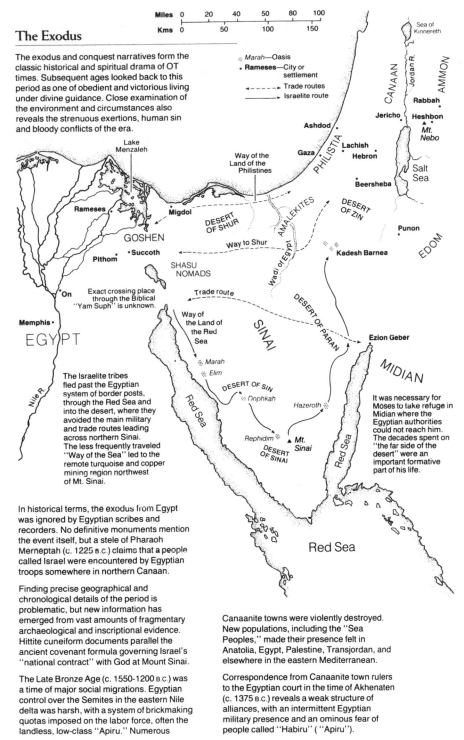

Miles 0   20   40   50   80   100
Kms 0   50   100   150

Marah—Oasis
Rameses—City or settlement
Trade routes
Israelite route

Sea of Kinnereth

CANAAN   Jordan R.   AMMON

Rabbah

Jericho   Heshbon
Mt. Nebo

Ashdod

Gaza   Lachish   Hebron

PHILISTIA

Salt Sea

Beersheba

Lake Menzaleh

Way of the Land of the Philistines

AMALEKITES

DESERT OF ZIN

Punon

Rameses   Migdol

DESERT OF SHUR

GOSHEN

Way to Shur

Kadesh Barnea

EDOM

Succoth
Pithom

SHASU NOMADS

Wadi of Egypt

On

Exact crossing place through the Biblical "Yam Suph" is unknown.

Trade route

DESERT OF PARAN

Memphis

Way of the Land of the Red Sea

SINAI

Ezion Geber

EGYPT

Nile R.

Marah
Elim

DESERT OF SIN

MIDIAN

The Israelite tribes fled past the Egyptian system of border posts, through the Red Sea and into the desert, where they avoided the main military and trade routes leading across northern Sinai. The less frequently traveled "Way of the Sea" led to the remote turquoise and copper mining region northwest of Mt. Sinai.

Dophkah

Hazeroth

Red Sea

Rephidim   Mt. Sinai
DESERT OF SINAI

Red Sea

It was necessary for Moses to take refuge in Midian where the Egyptian authorities could not reach him. The decades spent on "the far side of the desert" were an important formative part of his life.

Red Sea

In historical terms, the exodus from Egypt was ignored by Egyptian scribes and recorders. No definitive monuments mention the event itself, but a stele of Pharaoh Merneptah (c. 1225 B.C.) claims that a people called Israel were encountered by Egyptian troops somewhere in northern Canaan.

Finding precise geographical and chronological details of the period is problematic, but new information has emerged from vast amounts of fragmentary archaeological and inscriptional evidence. Hittite cuneiform documents parallel the ancient covenant formula governing Israel's "national contract" with God at Mount Sinai.

The Late Bronze Age (c. 1550-1200 B.C.) was a time of major social migrations. Egyptian control over the Semites in the eastern Nile delta was harsh, with a system of brickmaking quotas imposed on the labor force, often the landless, low-class "Apiru." Numerous

Canaanite towns were violently destroyed. New populations, including the "Sea Peoples," made their presence felt in Anatolia, Egypt, Palestine, Transjordan, and elsewhere in the eastern Mediterranean.

Correspondence from Canaanite town rulers to the Egyptian court in the time of Akhenaten (c. 1375 B.C.) reveals a weak structure of alliances, with an intermittent Egyptian military presence and an ominous fear of people called "Habiru" ("Apiru").

against their leaders and claimed God no longer cared for them. But God cared very much for them. He brought them to Mount Sinai and gave them His Law—the Ten Commandments. The Ten Commandments summarized the moral law. God also gave them a civil code to show how to maintain law and order and establish a system of government. And He gave them ceremonial laws which outlined how to perform animal sacrifices, when to observe holy days, and what should be considered clean and unclean food, among other things. The sacrificial system was, in fact, part of Israel's "means of grace" by which God would forgive their sins in anticipation of the once-for-all sacrifice of Christ.

Some people spend little time studying the ceremonial laws because Jesus abolished them by His death on the cross (Colossians 2:16–17; Mark 12:33). Few are interested in the civil laws because we live under a government different from the one to which Israel was called. But no one can ignore the moral law. It is the same today as it was then. We are aware of its continuing importance because Jesus points to it and upholds it.

When we read Exodus through Deuteronomy we learn how God loved His people and wanted to help them despite their sins. He fulfilled His promise to bring them to the Promised Land. Through Israel's journey we are reminded of God's promise to send a Savior to live, die, and rise again to bring us to the Promised Land of heaven.

An Overview

Read Exodus 3; 19:1–20:20; Numbers 13:17–14:25; and Deuteronomy 34.

The Message in Brief

The four readings include Moses' call to be Israel's deliverer from Egypt, the arrival of Israel at Mount Sinai, where they receive the Ten Commandments, Israel's lack of trust in God's providence and subsequent punishment, which forces them to wander in the wilderness for 40 years, and Moses' death after he sees the Promised Land.

Working with the Text
God Calls Moses (Exodus 3)

1. What does this chapter tell us about Moses' occupation when he received his call? Describe how God first presented Himself to Moses.

2. According to verse 6, whose God is God? Notice what tense is used to describe Him. What does this suggest about Abraham, Isaac, and Jacob's ongoing existence?

3. When Moses asks for God's name, what name does He give? Now look up John 8:58. What was Jesus saying about Himself that provoked the Jews to stone Him?

4. How would God make Egypt "favorably disposed" towards Israel so that Israel would be able to leave Egypt? Would the people of Israel leave Egypt poor and needy or would they be adequately enriched? Why?

The Ten Commandments (Exodus 19:1–20:20)

1. How long did it take Israel to get to Mount Sinai after leaving Egypt (v. 1)? How were they to prepare for God's descent onto the mountain? How does this preparation imply Israel's sinfulness and God's holiness?

2. Describe the ways in which God's presence affected the appearance of the mountain.

3. List in your own words the Ten Commandments.

Israel Rebels (Numbers 13:17–14:25)

1. What sort of information were Israel's spies to ascertain in Canaan? After exploring Canaan, what two schools of thoughts about its conquest did the spies present? Which perspective demonstrated a trust in God's promises? Which school of thought did Israel accept?

2. As a consequence of Israel's unbelief, what did God want to do to most of the nation? How did Moses intercede to deliver his people from God's judgment? In what way is God's judgment modified? What is God's final punishment for Israel's grumbling and unbelief? See also Numbers 32:11–13.

Moses' Death (Deuteronomy 34)

1. From what mountain did Moses see the Promised Land? To whom had God promised this land? Would Moses be able to enter it? Which of the two original Israelite exiles allowed to enter the Promised Land (Numbers 14:30) became Moses' successor?

2. What kind of status is Moses given at the end of Deuteronomy? Who is described as being superior to Moses in Hebrews 3:1–6?

Applying the Message

1. What do you think makes a good leader? How would you compare Moses' traits to those of your ideal leader (Exodus 2:11–12; 3:11; 4:1, 10, 13)? What does the choice of Moses as leader tell us about God's way and our way?

2. How did Jesus show that the moral law continues today and includes more than the Ten Commandments might at first suggest? See Matthew 5:21–48. What are the rules by which Christians are to be guided in following God's commandments? See Matthew 22:37–39 and Romans 13:8–10.

3. How can people complain even when they have been richly blessed by the Lord? What does this suggest to you about people? Are we any different than the people of Israel in this respect?

4. How would you describe your own life as one which appears to be "wandering through the wilderness"? At times it may seem as if our lives are aimless and without meaning. What does God's activity among Israel suggest about His guidance and will throughout our lives?

Taking the Message Home

Review

Contemplate the four readings you have studied in this lesson. How can the experiences of Israel mirror our personal relationship with God?

Looking Ahead

Before the next session read Joshua 6, which details the fall of Jericho. Jericho was only one city conquered by Israel in the Promised Land. How would you describe the extent of Jericho's destruction?

Read also Judges 6. Reflect on the fact that Gideon was only one of a number of "judges" God raised to bring order to His people and protect them from their enemies.

Working Ahead

Choose one or more of the following to complete before the next session:

1. Think back to the last time you moved. What did it feel like to pack everything and relocate? How disruptive was it to place your "stuff" in a new setting? Consider these aspects in relation to the people of Israel as they settled in their new land.

2. Can any war be moral? Can it be God-pleasing to kill? Before meeting again, organize your thoughts about the role of warfare in history. Particularly think about the Fifth Commandment, "You shall not murder" in relation to God's command to destroy the Canaanites and occupy the Promised Land. Is God inconsistent? Or does He, by His actions, offer qualifications to the commandment?

3. Do you remember the promise God gave Abraham in Genesis 17:8? "The whole land of Canaan, where you are now an alien, I will give as an everlasting possession to you and your descendants after you." There are some today—both Jews and Christians—who view this verse as a reason for modern-day Israel to hold on to—and even expand—its occupied territory. They believe none of the land originally conquered by the Old Testament Israelites should be given back to Israel's 20th-century neighbors. Do you agree with this? Why or why not?

Did you know that the reason Moses wasn't allowed into the Promised Land is found in Numbers 20:1–12? When Israel was complaining they had no water, God promised Moses that if he spoke to a particular rock, water would rush out. But rather than speak to the rock, Moses struck the rock twice with his staff. So what's wrong with that? Moses didn't believe God's promise that Moses' word alone would cause water to flow. That act of unbelief cost Moses the opportunity to enter the Promised Land. How sad the consequences of unbelief!

Session 4

Living in a New Land

Joshua 6; Judges 6; Ruth 4

Approaching This Study

We can only imagine how confused many of the people of Israel felt following the death of Moses. Almost all the Israelites knew nothing but a wilderness existence under Moses' leadership. Although they had been taught that God would bring them to a new and wonderful land, they had not yet seen it and could hardly imagine the thought of settling in any one place. But the Lord chose Joshua to continue leading His people, promising that through Joshua's guidance God would deliver the Promised Land to the people of Israel.

But the Promised Land wasn't vacant. It was occupied by various tribes of Canaanites. The book of Joshua details Israel's crossing of the Jordan River into Canaan and depicts Israel's victories in central, southern, and northern Canaan. The book ends with the land being distributed to the various tribes of Israel.

The book of Judges covers Israel's history from the death of Joshua until the reign of the first king of Israel. It was a chaotic period in Israel's history because there was no real governmental authority and because the people continually rebelled against God's authority. People could do pretty much as they pleased. As a result there was much crime, murder, robbery, even civil war. This situation existed for about 300 years. Frequently, the Lord would raise up a "judge," chosen by God to lead His people against foreign oppressors. Once the people were free again, they looked to their "judge" to help protect their rights. Altogether there were 12 judges, one of them a woman. The last judge, Samuel, helped Israel acquire its first king.

During the time of the judges, there was a woman named Ruth who was willing to leave her homeland and move to the land of Israel because she cared deeply for her mother-in-law. Her husband had died, but she was willing to give up her religion and follow the true God of

Exodus and the Conquest of Canaan

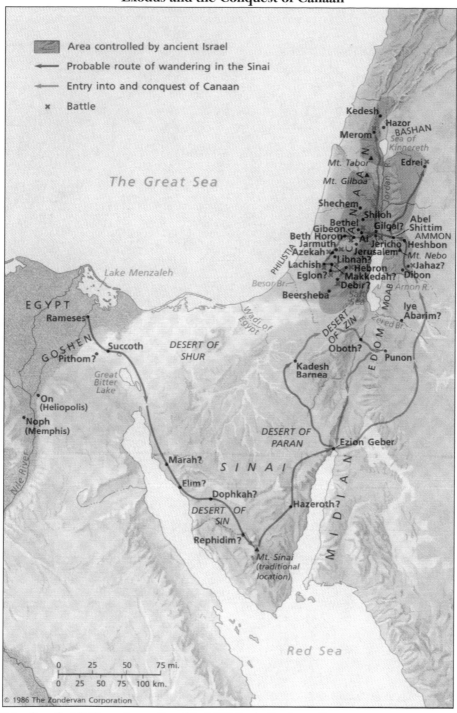

Taken from the NIV STUDY BIBLE. Copyright © 1985 by the Zondervan Corporation.
Used by permission of Zondervan Publishing House.

Land of the Twelve Tribes

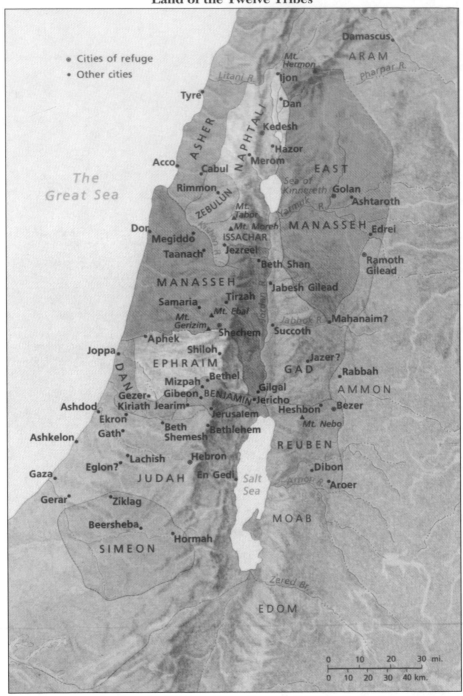

Taken from the NIV STUDY BIBLE. Copyright © 1985 by the Zondervan Corporation.
Used by permission of Zondervan Publishing House.

Israel. Even though Ruth was not a Jew, she became one of Jesus' ancestors. The four-chapter story of Ruth endears its reader to Ruth because of her loyalty and faithfulness to the Lord.

An Overview

We will be reading one chapter from Joshua, Judges, and Ruth. Although this will by no means cover all the details of each book, it will provide an overview of the main themes and ideas presented by the writings.

The Message in Brief

Joshua and Judges continue Israel's history after Moses' death. Joshua depicts the various conquests of the Promised Land. Judges describes the 300 years that follow, depicting an ongoing cycle that revolves around unbelief, oppression, cries of distress, and God's gracious deliverance. Ruth is the story of two women who find peace and security through the actions of a "kinsman-redeemer." This redemption foreshadows the deliverance Jesus would win for all people through His death on the cross.

Working with the Text
Joshua 6: Let the Walls Fall Down!

1. Moses was dead. Joshua had been chosen by God to lead the people of Israel. The people of Israel carried with them the ark of the covenant, a chest made of acacia wood which housed the tablets upon which were inscribed the Ten Commandments. Upon Joshua's command, the priests, carrying the ark of the covenant, walked into the Jordan River. When their feet touched the river, the waters parted and the people of Israel crossed into Canaan. Of what miracle does this remind you? See Exodus 14:21–31. How do you think this miracle confirmed Joshua as Moses' successor?

2. The first city inhabited by the Canaanites was Jericho. The name "Jericho" probably means "moon city," indicating the kind of pagan reli-

gion observed by its inhabitants. Describe in your own words the maneuvers God instructed Israel to perform in order to destroy Jericho's formidable walls.

3. What did God command concerning the articles of silver, gold, bronze, and iron in the city? How were the "living things" within the city devoted to God?

4. What curse did Joshua inflict on Jericho? Now look up 1 Kings 16:34 and explain how this curse was fulfilled!

Judges 6: Gideon's Call

1. As the chapter opens, we read about the oppression endured by the people of Israel. Why did this oppression come about? Who was oppressing God's people? What did they do to the Israelites? To whom did this oppression force the Israelites to turn?

2. Describe how the angel of the Lord first appeared to Gideon. Does the manner of his appearance surprise you? Why or why not? What was Gideon's response to the angel?

3. Why was Gideon hesitant to follow the Lord's call? How does Gideon's hesitation remind you of Moses?

4. Look particularly at verses 25 and 26. What particularly offensive sin had Israel committed? Gideon followed the Lord's command. Describe the courage he demonstrated. What does verse 27 suggest?

5. Gideon wasn't all that confident about his power to deliver God's people from the Midianites. Describe the two "tests" by which he hoped to determine the certainty of God's promises.

Ruth 4: Boaz, the Redeemer

Some background information, please! Ruth was not an Israelite. She was from the land of Moab. The Moabites were not descendants of Abraham like the Israelites. The Moabites were descendants of Lot (who was Abraham's nephew). So Ruth was not really one of the "chosen people." Nevertheless, she married an Israelite. But her husband died. And her mother in law was also a widow.

When Ruth's husband died, her mother-in-law, Naomi, urged Ruth to return to her homeland. But Ruth cared deeply for Naomi and would not leave her. Together they returned to Bethlehem in the land of the Israelites. Fortunately, Naomi had a wealthy in-law named Boaz. God guided Ruth to glean the leftover grain in Boaz's fields. Boaz noticed her and admired her. One evening Naomi directed Ruth to wait until Boaz was asleep. Then she was to lie at his feet. When he discovered Ruth, she called on him for help because he was a "kinsman-redeemer."

Now what is that? A kinsmen-redeemer was a relative who would pay a price to "redeem" or "buy back" a relative in need. How does Boaz redeem Naomi and Ruth? He buys back Naomi's land, marries Ruth, and fathers a son through Ruth to keep the family line alive.

Remember, in Ruth's day two widowed women were not highly valued. They were often defenseless and alone. To be delivered from this sad fate by a "kinsman-redeemer" was a great gift. Now read Ruth chapter 4 again.

There was a kinsman-redeemer even closer to Ruth than Boaz. He would have first rights to redeem a relative. So Boaz brought ten elders from the town and together they sat at the town gate. The town gate was Israel's version of the "town hall," where business and legal transactions took place. The 10 elders comprised a full court for legal proceedings.

At first, this unnamed kinsman-redeemer wanted to purchase Naomi's land. But then he realized his "redemption" would require marrying Ruth. Now this was a problem because should she give birth to his son, the kinsman-redeemer's property could be given back to the family of Naomi's husband. Is this getting complicated? Suffice to say that Boaz was not threatened by the possible loss of his property to another family after his death because of his love and compassion for Ruth. So when the other kinsman-redeemer declined purchasing Naomi's property, Boaz rushed in and redeemed the land, marrying Ruth in the bargain.

1. Now, look at Ruth 4:7. Describe how transactions were legalized in Ruth's day.

2. What was Ruth's son named? Who would be Ruth's great grandson?

Notice how Boaz was a "redeemer" who lived in Bethlehem. Jesus would also be born in Bethlehem and became the Redeemer of the world, buying people back from sin, death, and the devil. So, you see, Boaz foreshadowed or was a "type" of Jesus Christ!

Applying the Message

1. Feel free to express your opinion of the manner in which the Israelites "sacrificed" Jericho to God. Can you think of a reason this kind of destruction could be justified?

2. The story surrounding Gideon is a perfect example of the behavior of fallen human beings. They drift away from God. As a result, they find themselves in trouble. The trouble becomes so severe that they return to the Lord, calling on Him for help. In His great mercy He forgives and delivers. But, in that deliverance, the people become smug and sinful, straying once again from the will and Word of God. And so the cycle continues. In what way do you see that cycle occurring in your own life? Can you see it happening in American society? Explain.

3. The custom of a "kinsman-redeemer" seems foreign to contemporary people. It involves one person's sacrifice for the deliverance of another. But is it really so foreign? How can the principle of a "kinsman-redeemer" be seen in the following examples:

a. A mother or father declines a lucrative job because it would require too much time away from the family.

b. A teacher spends her spare time tutoring a student who is experiencing a particularly difficult time learning a subject.

c. A soldier throws himself on a grenade so that his comrades will not be killed.

d. Jesus dies on a cross so that others might not suffer eternal death.

Taking the Message Home

Review

Although Joshua and Judges are rather long books, the book of Ruth consists of only four chapters. Read the entire book before the next session and ponder its significance in terms of Jesus' death and resurrection.

Looking Ahead

In the next session we will examine Israel's first three kings: Saul, David, and Solomon. Read 1 Samuel 8:1–22 and consider why the people of Israel wanted a king. Was it a good idea? What did the Lord warn would happen? How did Israel's desire for a king demonstrate their lack of faith in God?

Working Ahead

Before the next session, consider the role of kings today. Are there any left? Why have many countries in the world abandoned this position of leadership? If you were faced with the option of anarchy or the coronation of a king, which would you choose?

Did you know that Matthew, in his Gospel, lists Ruth in the genealogy that traces Jesus' ancestry back to Abraham? Her name is found in Matthew 1:5. The Gospel writer Luke lists Boaz in his genealogy which traces Jesus' ancestry back to Adam. His name is found in Luke 3:32. So even though Ruth was not of Hebrew ancestry, she and Boaz are an important link in the genealogy between Abraham and Jesus.

Session 5

The Last Judge and the First Three Kings of Israel

1 Samuel 8; 13:1–15; 2 Samuel 11; 1 Kings 3:1–15

Approaching This Study

The people of Israel were ruled by judges for many years. Throughout this time they had to learn and relearn to trust in God's ability to raise up proper leaders and prophets from among them. The last judge to lead Israel was Samuel. He was a faithful servant of the Lord and boldly helped Israel defeat her enemies, particularly the Philistines. Unfortunately, Samuel's sons, whom Samuel appointed to succeed him as judges, were not God-fearing. They made the people of Israel unhappy by their willingness to pervert justice and accept bribes. So the people of Israel decided they no longer wanted judges to lead them. They wanted a king to rule them. They looked at how neighboring countries were ruled by kings and believed a king would be beneficial. Samuel tried to warn them of their folly, explaining that a king would conscript their sons into the military and force their daughters to work as royal servants. The people were not persuaded. When Samuel prayed about this matter to the Lord, God indicated that Israel was rebelling against Him. So He allowed them to face the consequences of their hardened will. They would be ruled by a king.

Saul was their first king. At first it seemed Israel would benefit by the rule of this God-fearing king. Saul led his people to military victory. But, as Lord Acton once wrote, "Power tends to corrupt and absolute power corrupts absolutely." Saul began to think he was above the laws of God and had a right to break them. God regretted choosing Saul as king and finally rejected him. As the Lord withdrew from Saul, Saul became more corrupt, violent, and paranoid. He even ordered the execution of God's priests and tried to kill his own son, Jonathan.

Jonathan became great friends with the shepherd David, chosen by

God to succeed Saul. David impressed the people of Israel when he challenged and killed the Philistine giant Goliath. After David was anointed king, only the people from his own tribe of Judah followed him for seven and a half years while the rest of the tribes followed one of Saul's sons. But David's power grew until all the tribes of Israel finally recognized him as their king. He was not a perfect king. He, like all of us, was a sinner. Still, the Lord forgave David and made him a great leader and warrior. He generally had a strong sense of fairness and a desire for justice. Under David the people of Israel became a great nation.

Solomon was the third king. He is often considered the wisest man who ever lived. When the Lord promised to give Solomon anything he asked for, Solomon asked for wisdom. The Lord was so impressed by Solomon's selfless request, He gave him riches and honor as well. King Solomon was a great builder. He built a magnificent temple for the Lord and a beautiful palace for himself. He built his own navy and erected various towns. Under Solomon, Israel seemed to enjoy its "golden age." But as Solomon grew older, he strayed from the Lord. Under the influence of his many foreign wives, his devotion to the true God became tarnished by the worship of false gods. As a result, God promised to split his nation and give most of it to someone else.

An Overview

This session incorporates four readings. One relates to Samuel's life, one to King Saul's, one to David, and one to Solomon. By examining the four incidents, readers can reflect on some of the important elements in the lives of these biblical figures and God's work in and through them. Read 1 Samuel 8 and 13:1–15; 2 Samuel 11; and 1 Kings 3:1–15.

The Message in Brief

The last judge, Samuel, warns God's people against the anointing of a king. He predicts that a king will exploit Israel. Nevertheless, the people of Israel demand one. After Samuel anoints Saul as king over Israel, Saul wages war on the Philistines. In a moment of fear and weakness, he loses confidence in God's will and promises, thereby demonstrating his faithlessness. David succeeds Saul as king of Israel, but even though he is considered the greatest of Israel's kings, he commits murder and adultery. As a result, his newborn child dies. David's next son, Solomon, becomes king of Israel after David's death. Solomon asks that the Lord grant him wisdom to rule God's people responsibly and fairly. Following this noble request, the Lord promises him wealth and honor as well.

David's Conquests

Once he had become king over all Israel (2Sa 5:1-5), David:

1. Conquered the Jebusite citadel of Zion/ Jerusalem and made it his royal city (2Sa 5:6-10);

2. Received the recognition of and assurance of friendship from Hiram of Tyre, king of the Phoenicians (2Sa 5:11-12);

3. Decisively defeated the Philistines so that their hold on Israelite territory was broken and their threat to Israel eliminated (2Sa 5:17-25; 8:1);

4. Defeated the Moabites and imposed his authority over them (2Sa 8:2);

5. Crushed the Aramean kingdoms of Hadadezer (king of Zobah), Damascus and Maacah and put them under tribute (2Sa 8:3-8; 10:6-19). Talmai, the Aramean king of Geshur, apparently had made peace with David while he was still reigning in Hebron and sealed the alliance by giving his daughter in marriage to David (2Sa 3:3; see 1Ch 2:23);

6. Subdued Edom and incorporated it into his empire (2Sa 8:13-14);

7. Defeated the Ammonites and brought them into subjection (2Sa 12:19-31);

8. Subjugated the remaining Canaanite cities that had previously maintained their independence from and hostility toward Israel, such as Beth Shan, Megiddo, Taanach and Dor.

Since David had earlier crushed the Amalekites (1Sa 30:17), his wars thus completed the conquest begun by Joshua and secured all the borders of Israel. His empire (united Israel plus the subjugated kingdoms) reached from Ezion Geber on the eastern arm of the Red Sea to the Euphrates River.

Working with the Text

1 Samuel 8: Samuel Warns against a King

1. According to verses 5 and 20, what are some of the reasons the elders of Israel wanted a king? How was this request in itself a sin against the Lord?

2. Describe the various troubles God predicted a king would inflict on Israel.

1 Samuel 13:1–15: A Good King Goes Bad

1. Saul's son, Jonathan, was bold and determined. He attacked a Philistine outpost, thereby threatening a powerful coastal enemy to the west. When the Philistines organized for battle, they vastly outnumbered King Saul's army. Their military even possessed the chariot, a weapon Israel would not acquire until the reign of King Solomon. Describe the men of Israel's reaction when they saw their enemies' forces.

2. After waiting on Samuel for seven days, Saul offered burnt offerings and fellowship offerings to the Lord. For this he was condemned as faithless. Why? To uncover Saul's sin, page back to 1 Samuel 10:8. What had Samuel commanded Saul to do with these offerings? What motivated Saul to act prematurely? How did Saul's action indicate faithlessness toward God? What would be the consequence of his sin?

2 Samuel 11: David and Bathsheba

1. The Lord entrusted David with royal power. How did David misuse this power after he saw Bathsheba bathing?

2. Describe the plan by which David hoped to hide his transgression from Uriah. What kept Uriah from fulfilling David's scheme?

3. In what way did David design the death of Uriah? Why was this scheme displeasing to the Lord? Now look at 2 Samuel 12:13–20. Did the Lord forgive David of his great sin? But there were still temporal consequences. What happened to David and Bathsheba's child?

1 Kings 3:1–15: Solomon's Request for Wisdom

1. Although Solomon would be a great king, what two grave weakness did he demonstrate early in his reign according to verses 1–3? For help in understanding Solomon's failings, look up Numbers 33:52 and 1 Kings 11:1–2.

2. We commonly describe Solomon's great gift as "wisdom." How is this "wisdom" defined by Solomon in verse 9? What do you think is the difference between "wisdom" and "knowledge?" Because of Solomon's selfless request, what other gifts did God promise him?

3. Much of 1 and 2 Chronicles covers the same historical period as 2 Samuel, and 1 and 2 Kings. But the reigns of David and Solomon are greatly idealized in the Chronicles. No mention is made, for example, of David's sin with Bathsheba. In the same way, no mention is made of Solomon's idolatry nor his foreign wives. Compare the description of Solomon's visit with the Queen of Sheba as recorded in 1 Kings 10:1–5 with 2 Chronicles 9:1–4 and note their similarities.

Applying the Message

1. Should people use the Bible to discover the best form of government? Why or why not? Is that what the Bible is for? Explain your answers.

2. Imagine yourself in King Saul's shoes. The Philistines have gathered their military might to bear down on your inferior army. Samuel, who is supposed to arrive within seven days and offer burnt offerings to the Lord is delayed. Your soldiers are frightened, quaking, hiding, and deserting. To bolster their courage, you offer the burnt offerings instead of Samuel—against God's wishes. It's easy to empathize with King Saul. Were we in his shoes, we would be tempted to act similarly. God, however, judges Saul severely. As a result of his faithlessness, God's favor is withdrawn and given to David. Why is God so very strict? After all, David would commit adultery and murder. But doesn't his punishment appear less severe? What do you think God is demonstrating by His response?

3. Isn't it somewhat remarkable to witness great King David acting as an adulterer and murderer? Initially, he refused to recognize the reality of his failings. The prophet, Nathan, was forced to confront David about his immoral actions. Only then did David recognize his sin

(2 Samuel 12). But isn't David like all fallen people? In what ways do we deny our wrongdoings? How do people rationalize their wickedness? Give some examples.

4. King Solomon's wisdom consisted in his ability to discern right from wrong. But look up 1 Kings 11:1–6. How many wives did Solomon possess? How many concubines? Solomon's relationships with a multitude of foreign women was clearly a violation of God's directive. And yet, the writer of Kings seems to criticize Solomon primarily for his growing tendency to worship false gods. Explain the relationship between these two offenses. What "foreign" influences might tempt you toward unfaithfulness?

Taking the Message Home

Review

When time allows, reread this session's passages relating to Samuel, Saul, David, and Solomon. Contemplate how each great biblical person suffered grave failings. Consider how the existence of sin creates "fatal flaws" in all of us. Then thank the Lord for His forgiving grace, and praise Him for the hope of eternal life won by Jesus' death and resurrection.

Looking Ahead

Before the next session read 1 Kings 12:1–17 to discover the reason for the split of God's people into two separate nations. After this division, the 10 northern tribes would be called Israel while the 2 southern tribes would be known as Judah. After reading this section, consider the two methods by which power can be maintained. One method is to serve, the other is to oppress. Which is to be desired? Why do you think so many leaders follow the road of oppression rather than servanthood?

Working Ahead

Complete one or more of the following before the next session:

1. Spend some time contemplating what would happen to American society if every Bible were to disappear tomorrow. Write some of the differences you think might evolve over the years. Be prepared to discuss your ideas at the next session.

2. Some people define America as a "Christian" nation. But what if we were suddenly to be subjected to an Islamic or Stalinist-style government, one which banned the Christian church? What if many of your Christian brothers and sisters were put to death? How would you find support in your faith? How would you feel about the Lord's guidance and protection?

Did you know that King Saul committed suicide after suffering defeat at the hands of the Philistines? When the Philistines found Saul's body, they cut off his head and stripped off his armor. 1 Samuel 31:10 says, "They put his armor in the temple of the Ashtoreth and fastened his body to the wall of Beth Shan." The University Museum of Pennsylvania uncovered in the ruins of Beth Shan, dating to 1000 B.C., the temple of Ashtoreth. This would be the same temple in which Saul's armor was hung as a sign of the Philistine victory!

Session 6

The Nation Falls Apart

1 Kings 12; 21; 2 Kings 22; 25

Approaching This Study

It wasn't long before the Golden Age of Israel came to an end. In fact, the nation of Israel divided immediately after Solomon's death. When Solomon's son, Rehoboam, became king, representatives from the people of Israel ask that he reduce the heavy taxes Solomon had placed on them. Rehoboam responded that his taxes would be even more burdensome. The result of Rehoboam's "hard-nosed" response was a split in the kingdom. Ten of the 12 tribes refused to honor him as king. They refused to pay his taxes or submit to his forced labor. Only the tribe of Judah and some of the Benjamites remained with him. And when Rehoboam prepared his military for war against the other tribes, God intervened and commanded he desist.

From then on, Israel would be two nations. One was the Northern Kingdom, called Israel. In Jesus' day, it would be known as Samaria. The first northern king was Jeroboam. The Southern Kingdom was called Judah. Rehoboam remained king of the Southern Kingdom and kept Jerusalem as his capital.

Down through the next several centuries, some of Judah's kings were faithful to God and others were not. In Israel, however, all the kings were evil. Some 250 years after Solomon's death, the people of the Northern Kingdom were taken into captivity by the Assyrians. The 10 tribes of Israel ceased to exist. Judah, on the other hand, continued for almost 150 years longer.

It was a rocky existence for Judah. Several evil kings succeeded in leading the people away from the Lord, but there were some God-fearing kings and prophets (most notably, the prophet Elijah) who worked to make the citizens of Judah recognize their sinful ways and repent. Such kings as Asa, Jehoshaphat, and Hezekiah obeyed the

Lord and attempted to rid the land of idolatry. But other kings like Ahaziah, Ahaz, and Manasseh destroyed the good that had been accomplished. The last great king of Judah was Josiah. He was only eight years old when he assumed the throne. As he grew older he destroyed the altars to false gods, began observing the Passover, put idolatrous priests to death, and brought back the Word of God. All the kings after him were evil.

The fall of Judah occurred slowly. Finally, however, the people of Judah were defeated and taken into captivity by the Babylonians. Jerusalem and its temple were destroyed. But remember, God had promised that the Messiah, Jesus Christ, would be born from the tribe of Judah and be a descendant of King David. Because God had selected Judah as the nation through which Christ would be born, the people were able to return from captivity and rebuild Jerusalem.

In this session we will look at the division that arose after Solomon's death. Next we will consider the great prophet Elijah as he dealt with an evil king, Ahab, and his wife, Jezebel. We will then consider the last great king of Judah, Josiah, and his faithful service to the Lord. Finally, we will focus on the destruction of Jerusalem by the Babylonians.

An Overview

Because this study is an overview of the Old Testament, many of the individual histories of kings and prophets must be overlooked. But these four suggested readings—1 Kings 12; 1 Kings 21; 2 Kings 22; 2 Kings 25—will give us an insight into the division among God's people, and an understanding of the wickedness of the Northern Kingdom in contrast to the faithfulness of some of Judah's kings. Each passage relates a story, and the chapters should be read one at a time by volunteers.

The Message in Brief

Nations weaken as they split in civil war. The division of Israel into two nations signaled the beginning of the end for the people of the Old Testament. Although it would take several generations, the fate of God's people was determined by their ongoing sin and faithlessness. We honor those kings and prophets who hoped to stem the tide against increasing corruption and skepticism. In the end, God would allow His people to be defeated and exiled, but not without the promise that one day a "new Israel" would rise up in the birth of God's Son, Jesus Christ, who would come to earth to save all people from their sins.

Working with the Text

The Nation is Divided (1 Kings 12)

1. Jeroboam was from the tribe of Ephraim. He was not from Solomon's tribe of Judah. The prophet Ahijah told Jeroboam that he would become king over 10 of Israel's tribes. So King Solomon grew afraid of Jeroboam, and tried to kill him, but Jeroboam fled to Egypt until Solomon's death. Once Solomon was gone, Jeroboam felt sufficiently secure to return and lead the 10 tribes who seceded from Israel. What prompted the secession? Might Solomon's son, Rehoboam, have maintained unity had he not been so stubborn? What did the 10 tribes do to Adoniram who was in charge of the forced labor? Which tribe refused to follow Jeroboam?

2. The Northern Kingdom immediately rejected the Lord. Why did Jeroboam establish a different priesthood, the worship of golden calves, and pagan shrines? How would this set the tone for the history of the Northern Kingdom?

Elijah vs. Ahab (1 Kings 21)

1. Perhaps the most wicked king of the Northern Kingdom was Ahab, accompanied by his wife, Jezebel. Ahab reigned some 50 years after Jeroboam, but the evil nature of the Northern Kingdom reached its zenith under his leadership. One such example involved his treatment of a vineyard owner, Naboth. What did Ahab want from Naboth? When Naboth refused to deliver his vineyard to Ahab, how did Jezebel resolve the situation?

2. The great prophet Elijah heard about Ahab's wicked deed. What was Elijah's prophesy concerning Ahab's and Jezebel's fates (v. 19)? Now look at 1 Kings 22:34–38. How was Elijah's prophecy about Ahab fulfilled? Also look at 2 Kings 9:30–37 and note again how Elijah's prophecy was fulfilled.

The Last Great King of Judah (2 Kings 22)

1. Josiah demonstrated his love for the Lord by repairing the temple. What happened during this restoration? What treasure was found? How did Josiah react to the incredible find?

2. When a prophetess named Huldah learned about the discovery, she spoke God's words of judgment and mercy. Against whom were her words of judgment directed? But who was shown mercy, and why? Now turn to 2 Kings 23:24–25 and describe Josiah's reign.

The End of a Nation (2 Kings 25)

1. It took 1,000 years of faithlessness and sin, but God's judgment was finally in order. Describe the events involved in Jerusalem's fall.

What happened to King Zedekiah? What did the Babylonians do to the temple and palace? What happened to the citizens of Jerusalem?

2. Interestingly, the book of 2 Kings does not end on a hopeless note. The king who had been deposed before Zedekiah and taken to Babylon is freed and cared for. The writer of 2 Kings concludes with the joyful release of Jehoiachin. What message did Jehoiachin's release convey in the midst of Jerusalem's miserable collapse?

Applying the Message

1. Can evil rulers hurt a nation? If so, in what way? Give examples, if possible. What do you think Christians can do about corrupt government officials?

2. Isn't it astounding that God's people could "lose" the Book of the Law? Yet that's precisely what happened in Judah by the time of King Josiah. Is it possible that in this day and age, when there exist more translations of the Bible than at any period in history, our church could "lose" God's Word? How? In order for God's Word to work, what must people do with it?

3. How does God continue to bless people today in spite of their wickedness? What does God's long patience evidence of His desire for all people?

Taking the Message Home

Review

Re-read the Bible passages studied in this session. Contemplate again the consequences of national immorality and reflect on how the individual Christian can be a positive, God-pleasing influence on the people she or he knows.

Looking Ahead

Before the next session, read Hosea 4:1–2, Amos 5:21–22, 8:4–6, and Micah 3:1–3. Get a sense of the rampant corruption evident as Israel and Judah fell apart. Are the people of our world any different? Then read Zephaniah 3:14, 20; Micah 4:1–5; and Joel 2:19–21. How did these prophets give people hope even though the ravages of sin continued to grow?

Working Ahead

Complete one or more of the following before the next session:

1. Gather newspaper clippings from a newspaper or weekly magazine that demonstrate the corruption present in the modern world. Be ready to share these stories with others at the beginning of the next session.

2. Reflect on the prophets of our day—those pastors and teachers who faithfully teach God's Word of Law and Gospel. Do many listen? Ask your pastor how he feels about the effectiveness of his message. What motivates him to continue speaking God's Word? How does he feel about the way it is received?

3. In your Bible's table of contents, look up the names of the books from Hosea to Malachi. Try to pronounce them. If you have trouble, use a Bible dictionary to discover the correct pronunciation.

Did you know that archaeologists have uncovered ancient Babylonian administrative tablets which record the payment of oil and barley rations to the prisoners held in Babylon. Some of these tablets mention Yaukin (Jehoiachin) king of Iahuda (Judah) and five of his sons. This is truly a dramatic archaeological confirmation of biblical history!

Session 7

Prophets Who Brought God's Message to Sinful People

1 Kings 19; 2 Kings 2; Hosea 8; Micah 3

Approaching This Study

During the years when Israel and Judah were disintegrating, few were interested in serving God. It was much easier to be selfish and greedy, exploiting the poor and helpless. When people suffered the consequences of their rebellious acts against God, they did not repent. They blamed God.

God sent His prophets. The prophets condemned the people's sinful ways and warned about God's impending judgment. But the prophets also reminded their listeners that God loved them despite their sin. The prophets looked to a future when the Lord would recall His people from exile to rebuild the nation to whom the Savior of the whole world would be born.

Elijah and Elisha are some of the best known prophets of this period. Elijah challenged the pagan prophets of Baal to determine whose god was sufficiently powerful to respond in fire. Elijah was the one who raised a widow's son from death to life, and it was Elijah who was taken to heaven in a fiery chariot. Elisha was Elijah's successor. Elisha was a fearless prophet who performed many different miracles and established a school for the training of prophets. Both Elijah and Elisha worked in the Northern Kingdom, where the kings were particularly evil. Very few people listened to them, but God sustained them even when the rulers sought to put them to death.

After Elijah and Elisha other prophets carried on the proclamation of God's Word. Some of them, like Isaiah, Jeremiah, and Ezekiel, are commonly called "the major prophets." Others, like Joel, Amos, Hosea, Micah, and Zephaniah, are called "the minor prophets." These categories are not meant to imply different levels of importance, but to recognize that the books of some prophets are much longer than others.

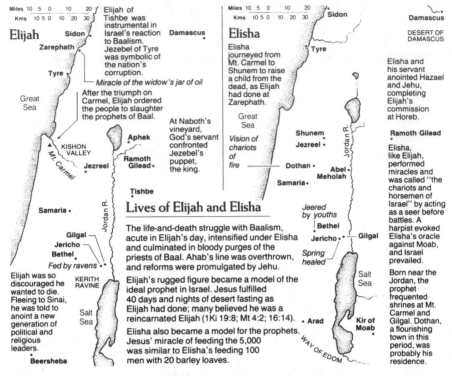

Elijah

Elijah of Tishbe was instrumental in Israel's reaction to Baalism. Jezebel of Tyre was symbolic of the nation's corruption.

Miracle of the widow's jar of oil

After the triumph on Carmel, Elijah ordered the people to slaughter the prophets of Baal.

At Naboth's vineyard, God's servant confronted Jezebel's puppet, the king.

Elijah was so discouraged he wanted to die. Fleeing to Sinai, he was told to anoint a new generation of political and religious leaders.

Elisha

Elisha journeyed from Mt. Carmel to Shunem to raise a child from the dead, as Elijah had done at Zarephath.

Vision of chariots of fire

Jeered by youths

Spring healed

Elisha and his servant anointed Hazael and Jehu, completing Elijah's commission at Horeb.

Elisha, like Elijah, performed miracles and was called "the chariots and horsemen of Israel" by acting as a seer before battles. A harpist evoked Elisha's oracle against Moab, and Israel prevailed.

Born near the Jordan, the prophet frequented shrines at Mt. Carmel and Gilgal. Dothan, a flourishing town in this period, was probably his residence.

Lives of Elijah and Elisha

The life-and-death struggle with Baalism, acute in Elijah's day, intensified under Elisha and culminated in bloody purges of the priests of Baal. Ahab's line was overthrown, and reforms were promulgated by Jehu.

Elijah's rugged figure became a model of the ideal prophet in Israel. Jesus fulfilled 40 days and nights of desert fasting as Elijah had done; many believed he was a reincarnated Elijah (1Ki 19:8; Mt 4:2; 16:14).

Elisha also became a model for the prophets. Jesus' miracle of feeding the 5,000 was similar to Elisha's feeding 100 men with 20 barley loaves.

The prophet Joel worked in Judah. He preached at a time when locusts had created a terrible famine. He used the locusts to describe how enemies would overwhelm God's people just as the locusts had devoured the fields.

The prophet Amos was a common man who earned his living from shepherding and from caring for a sycamore-fig grove. He prophesied about God's impending judgment against the extravagant indulgence, idolatry, immorality, and corruption prevalent before Israel's fall to the Assyrians.

Micah also predicted the fall of the Northern Kingdom, but lived somewhat later than Amos and saw many of his predictions fulfilled.

The prophet Hosea lived during the tragic final days of the Northern Kingdom. Greatly alarmed by the sins of the nation, Hosea warned that Israel would soon be gobbled up by Assyria.

Unlike Micah, Amos, and Hosea, Zephaniah enjoyed considerable social status in Judah. He may have been related to the royal line. Zephaniah's words show he was familiar with court circles and current political issues. He announced God's approaching judgment against Judah. Like many of the other prophets, Zephaniah ended his pronouncements on a positive note, emphasizing the future restoration of God's people.

Let's look at these various prophets of doom and deliverance who were sent by God to turn His people from their sinful ways. Their messages can be as timely to those living at the turn of the 21st century as they were to God's people more than 2,500 years ago.

An Overview

We will be reading events from the lives of Elijah and Elisha, while considering some selected words from Hosea and Micah. Elijah and Elisha are two of the greatest prophets of the Old Testament. The prophecies of Hosea and Micah reflect words of judgment and hope prevalent among the prophets called by God to warn about Israel and Judah's fall. Read about Elijah in 1 Kings 19. Then read about Elijah's successor, Elisha, in 2 Kings 2. What similarities and differences do you find between the two great prophets? Finally, read Hosea 8 and Micah 3.

The Message in Brief

These four selections should provide a "feel" for the role of the prophets during this period of Israel and Judah's history. Be sure to notice how the words and actions of the prophets were not intended simply to predict the future, but rather to proclaim God's words of judgment and deliverance. The prophets were moved to stand as God's ambassador against hostile and abusive enemies for the purpose of persuading as many as possible to turn from their sinful ways. Many of the prophets' messages resemble each other, but the fact that God raised up several different people to proclaim similar themes during the same period of time indicates how important He considered His communication and the depth of His love for His people. God's promise of deliverance points to the ultimate deliverance God provided through the life, death, and resurrection of His Son.

Working with the Text
Elijah (1 Kings 19)

1. Remember Jezebel? She was Ahab's wife, the evil queen of Israel. Because Elijah had demonstrated God's great power over her pagan

god, Baal, Jezebel was determined to kill the prophet. She even warned Elijah about her intent! How did Elijah react to her threat? Describe the depth of his despair. The Lord appeared to strengthen and sustain him. What was the first thing God's angel gave Elijah?

2. Elijah complained that he was the only follower of God left. How did God respond to this complaint? Describe the different ways God then demonstrated His power over the forces of nature. But in what fashion did the Lord appear? According to God's count, how many believers were left in Israel?

3. Describe how Elijah called Elisha. How did Elisha underscore that his call was permanent?

Elisha (2 Kings 2)

1. After reading verses 1–6, how would you describe Elisha's loyalty to Elijah? When Elijah and Elisha reached the Jordan River, what did Elijah do? Of whom does this remind you? See Exodus 14:21–22 and Joshua 3:6–17. What does this suggest about Elijah? When Elisha returned to the Jordan, what did he do according to verse 14? What does this suggest about Elisha's upcoming role?

2. Describe the manner in which Elijah was taken to heaven. Later, 50 men searched for Elijah. Did they find him? Why not?

3. Notice how one of Elisha's earliest miracles involved purifying the waters near Jericho. He took a bowl of salt and threw it into the spring. The waters of the spring became wholesome and fresh. Now turn back to Exodus 15:22–25. How does Elisha's act resemble Moses' act? Take a peek at Numbers 18:19 and 2 Chronicles 13:5. What might have been the significance of Elisha using salt to perform his miracle?

4. What did the offensive youth from Bethel call Elisha? Which commandment did they break by their actions? What was the consequence of their disobedience?

Hosea (Hosea 8)

1. One of the interesting things about studying God's words of judgment against His people is our ability to decipher the sins which were being committed. As you read through this chapter, list the different ways Israel disobeyed God.

2. What does God warn will happen to the nation because of its apostasy?

Micah (Micah 3)

1. Micah's prophecy contains more words of judgment, this time against the leaders of Judah. Describe the various ways the so-called leaders of God's people have strayed from the Lord. How are their words giving Judah a false sense of security? Considering what Judah's leaders are telling the people, how do you think Micah's words were received?

2. According to verse 8, what is Micah's role as prophet? How is he strengthened in the face of his enemies' hostility? Because of the many false prophets flourishing in Judah, what will God do with the gift of prophecy according to verse 6? How is that prophecy echoed by Amos in 8:11?

3. Finally, turn to Zephaniah 3:14–20. With what words of encouragement does the prophet end his message? How is this prophecy of forgiveness, mercy, and hope reflected by the other prophets in Hosea 14:4–7; Joel 3:18–21; Amos 9:11–15; and Micah 7:18–20?

Applying the Message

1. Sometimes the Christian can feel very much alone in his or her faith. Particularly during periods of emotional or spiritual stress, the Christian can be tempted to think that no one cares. It can be of some comfort to know great prophets such as Elijah experienced similar feel-

ings. How can God's response to Elijah be of comfort to us today? Where can we find people to support us in our journey of faith?

2. Consider the drama involved with God's approach to Elijah. Elijah experienced a fierce wind, followed by a violent earthquake and a blazing fire. But God's voice came as a gentle whisper. What does this suggest to you about God's ability to comfort those who feel their lives are unstable and out of control?

3. Remember how Elijah called Elisha into the prophetic ministry? How is Elijah's action imitated today when a pastor is ordained into the ministry.

Taking the Message Home

Review

As you reflect on the prophets' ministries, consider the difficulties Christians face when they are witnesses to the simple truth of God's Word. How will people react? Will there be good as well as unpleasant responses?

Looking Ahead

As accurate as this session's prophets were in predicting the demise of Israel and Judah and the eventual restoration of God's people, there were two prophets—Isaiah and Jeremiah—who more clearly foresaw an even greater event: the coming of the Messiah. Before the next session, read Isaiah 53 and contemplate some possible ways this chapter was fulfilled in the person and through the work of Jesus Christ.

Working Ahead

There are several figures today who are considered great "prophets" or evangelists of the Lord. Some of them are on the radio, some on television. Before the next session, consider some of these individuals. If the prophet's primary responsibility is to alert persons to their state of sin so that they turn to God's grace and forgiveness in Jesus Christ, who would you consider the greatest prophet today?

Did you know that the prophet Elijah, taken away in a fiery chariot, would return again? In the gospels relating Jesus' life, Elijah returns with Moses and Jesus on the Mount of Transfiguration, discussing Jesus' upcoming journey to Jerusalem, where He would suffer and die for the sins of the world. Elijah and Moses disappeared as suddenly as they had appeared. The three disciples who witnessed this—Peter, James, and John—were terrified. But Jesus comforted them and told them not to fear. See Matthew 17:1–13; Mark 9:2–13; and Luke 9:28–36.

Session 8

Two Great Prophets

2 Kings 19; Isaiah 53, Jeremiah 1; Lamentations 1:1–10

Approaching This Study

Every so often tabloid newspapers print the predictions of modern "seers." Only occasionally, by coincidence, do one of these predictions come true.

In contrast to modern "seers," the prophets Isaiah and Jeremiah were consistently accurate in their predictions about the future. Isaiah, for example, foresaw a kingdom beyond Israel or Judah, a kingdom which would be greater than anything the world had ever known. He predicted the coming of God's kingdom in Jesus Christ. Hundreds of years before Jesus was born, Isaiah described Jesus' birth, life, and suffering. One can only marvel at the clarity of Isaiah's vision. It was as if Isaiah was standing at the foot of the cross when Jesus died for the sins of the world.

Isaiah lived during a period when Israel's descendants were only pretending to worship the true God. They had strayed far from the path God had intended, and Isaiah had to warn them about their hypocrisy and faithlessness. He wasn't afraid to tell them the truth about their erring ways. To get a sense of Isaiah's blunt honesty, consider Isaiah 1:10–17.

Jeremiah's prophetic ministry occurred during a period when things were even worse. The nation of Judah was clearly headed for destruction; yet many false prophets kept assuring God's people they had nothing to worry about. In fact, no one wanted to hear Jeremiah's honest words of judgment from God. When he wrote his prophecies on a scroll, the king cut up the scroll and burned it. Many accused Jeremiah of rebelling against the government. They imprisoned the prophet and tried to kill him. But he continued to proclaim God's Word. Jeremiah was an eyewitness to the fall of Jerusalem in 586 B.C. Many believe he wrote Lamentations, a book which mourns the destruction of the city.

These two great prophets, Isaiah and Jeremiah, kept preaching even

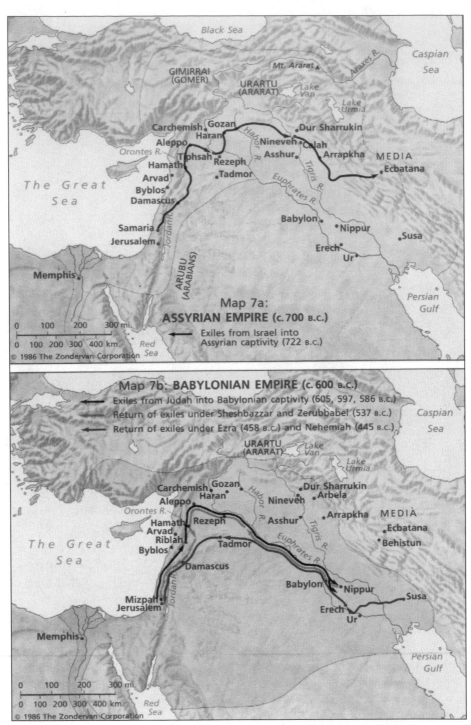

Map 7a:
ASSYRIAN EMPIRE (c. 700 B.C.)
→ Exiles from Israel into Assyrian captivity (722 B.C.)
© 1986 The Zondervan Corporation

Map 7b: BABYLONIAN EMPIRE (c. 600 B.C.)
→ Exiles from Judah into Babylonian captivity (605, 597, 586 B.C.)
→ Return of exiles under Sheshbazzar and Zerubbabel (537 B.C.)
→ Return of exiles under Ezra (458 B.C.) and Nehemiah (445 B.C.)
© 1986 The Zondervan Corporation

when most of the people refused to listen. Despite all the evil around them and the certain judgment to come, they promised that someday God's people would return to their homeland and rebuild. God still loved His people. He continually called them to look forward to the coming of a Messiah, Jesus Christ.

An Overview

Have one volunteer read the story of the siege of Jerusalem by the Assyrians in 2 Kings 19. Notice the important role given Isaiah. Then read Isaiah's prediction about the "Suffering Servant" in Isaiah 53. As it is read, look for the ways in which it describes Jesus' ministry. Have a third individual read Jeremiah 1 and consider Jeremiah's reluctance to enter the prophetic ministry. Finally, have someone read Lamentations 1:1–10 and reflect on the horror of Jerusalem's fall to the Babylonians.

The Message in Brief

The readings for this session begin with the siege of Jerusalem by King Sennacherib and the Assyrian nation. As God's people endure the siege, Isaiah counsels Jerusalem to wait for the Lord's intervention. God's miraculous intervention occurs when Sennacherib's armies are destroyed in one night by the angel of death. Later, in Isaiah 53, the prophet foresees the sacrificial death of God's Suffering Servant. He details God's plan of salvation, that is, how an innocent Jesus would take the sins of the world and die so that all people could gain His perfection and "rightness" in God's eyes.

As we consider Jeremiah, we will gain an appreciation for his reluctance to serve God as a prophet. Then we will ponder the prophet's sorrowful description of the fall of Jerusalem.

Working with the Text
The Siege of Jerusalem (2 Kings 19)

1. Let's go back more than 100 years before the fall of Jerusalem to the Babylonians. Israel had fallen to the Assyrians. Twenty years after the fall of the Northern Kingdom, the Assyrians had conquered most of the Southern Kingdom and were besieging its capital, Jerusalem. In 701 B.C. the Assyrian king, Sennacherib, surrounded the city, taunting its citizens with the prospect of imminent destruction. Jerusalem's king, Hezekiah, and the city's citizens were horrified. Hezekiah tore his

clothes and put on sackcloth and ashes as a sign of penitence. Hezekiah desperately wanted the Lord's intervention, so he sent his officials to talk to the prophet Isaiah. What did Isaiah tell Hezekiah in 2 Kings 19:7? Did Sennacherib think Israel's God was to be feared? Why? See verses 10–13. What did God promise concerning Sennacherib's attempt to defeat Judah (vv. 32–33)?

2. How did God fulfill His promise to Hezekiah and the residents of Jerusalem (35–37)? During what event did the Lord act in a similar fashion (Exodus 12:12–13)?

The Suffering Servant (Isaiah 53)

The book of Isaiah includes four prophecies concerning a "Suffering Servant." In a general sense, these prophecies could refer to the people of Israel. But as they unfold, it becomes evident that more than Israel is envisioned. As chapter 53 proceeds, the reader is drawn inevitably to the suffering and death of Jesus Christ. Compare the following prophecies to Jesus' ministry:

1. Isaiah 53:3 and Matthew 16:21; 27:27–31

2. Isaiah 53:4–6 and 1 Peter 2:24; Romans 4:25; 2 Corinthians 5:21

3. Isaiah 53:7 and Mark 14:53–61

4. Isaiah 53:9 and Mark 15:25–27; Matthew 27:57–60

5. Isaiah 53:12 and Philippians 2:5–11

Jeremiah's Call (Jeremiah 1)

1. When did God choose Jeremiah to be His prophet?

2. How did Jeremiah respond to his call? Was he eager and willing? Why or why not?

3. What does Jeremiah learn about the future of Jerusalem and the towns of Judah? This would indeed be frightening news to the residents of Jerusalem. They would hate Jeremiah for proclaiming it. But why could Jeremiah be bold in proclaiming the Lord's judgment? Who would protect him?

Mourning Jerusalem's Fall (Lamentations 1:1–10)

The author of Lamentations never really identifies himself. The style and vocabulary of Jeremiah and Lamentations are similar. Since Jeremiah was an eyewitness to Jerusalem's fall, scholars often ascribe Lamentations to Jeremiah's pen. According to verse 3, what has happened to the nation of Judah? What does verse 7 say about the fate of Jerusalem? And what happened to Jerusalem's treasures according to verse 10?

Applying the Message

1. The story of God's miraculous intervention to deliver Jerusalem from Sennacherib is inspiring. As you review your life, can you remember moments when the Lord protected you from danger? Share these experiences with the rest of the participants.

2. Read again Isaiah 53:5. Explain in your own words the "substitution" involved in Jesus' death. For whom was He pierced? For what reason was He crushed? What did His punishment bring us? And what is the result of His wounds? Knowing the reason and result of Jesus' suffering, how do you respond?

3. It's fascinating to learn that God had a plan for Jeremiah before he was conceived or born. What does this suggest about your life? When was that purpose known to God? When an abortion is committed, what effect does it have on God's will?

4. When you read Lamentations, you may be overwhelmed by the depth of the loss experienced by the writer. And yet, in the middle of the book, the author focuses on the goodness of God. Our Lord is the God of hope, love, faithfulness, and salvation. His compassion never fails. Why might this be a good book to read the next time you feel discouraged or overwhelmed by life's troubles?

Taking the Message Home

Review

As time permits, read again Isaiah 53 and Jeremiah 1. Reflect on the remarkable clarity of Isaiah's vision and Jeremiah's prophecy of invasion by Babylon. Then pray the Lord continues to safeguard His people from evil.

Looking Ahead

Before the next session read Daniel 6 and Esther 2. Both record events that occurred during the exile of God's people. Consider how God accompanied His people to a foreign land and continued to watch over them.

Working Ahead

Complete one or more of the following before the next session:

1. What would you do if your country were occupied by a foreign power? Would you try to leave and find a new life elsewhere, or would you remain and try to bring God's Word to others? How could you keep your faith in God? List ways you would sustain and grow in faith despite the adversity.

2. What would be your reaction if you were ordered to obey a command contrary to your religious beliefs? What if you were told you would be put to death if you refused? Do you think you would continue to witness to the Lord, or would you hide your faith from public view?

Did you know that at one time, some liberal scholars believed the story of Jerusalem's siege by Sennacherib was a myth? However, archaeologists uncovered a clay prism in the ruins of Nineveh which Sennacherib had made. It was a record of some of his battles. The annals note: "As for Hezekiah the Jew, he did not submit to my yoke. I laid siege to 46 of his strong cities, walled forts and to the countless small villages in their vicinity, and conquered them by means of well-stamped earth ramps and battering-rams brought near to the walls combined with the attack by foot soldiers, using mines, breaches as well as sapper work. I drove out 200,150 people, young and old, male and female, horses, mules, donkeys, camels, big and small cattle beyond counting and considered them booty. Hezekiah himself I made a prisoner in Jerusalem, his royal residence, like a bird in a cage."

Sennacherib's account of the conflict differs from that of the Bible. Naturally, the Assyrian king neglected to record the disastrous massacre of his men by the angel of death!

Session 9

God's People Living in a Foreign Land

Ezekiel 5; Daniel 5; Esther 2:1–18

Approaching This Study

After Israel split into two smaller kingdoms, both kingdoms continued for more than 250 years. During this time, God sent prophets to preach His Word to encourage His people to repent. Few people listened. They were busy with other concerns and were not interested in hearing. As time went by their faith grew weaker. Finally, the king of Assyria overran the Northern Kingdom. The Southern Kingdom lasted another 135 years because several God-fearing figures helped stem the tide of faithlessness. Nonetheless, Judah was finally conquered as well, this time by the Babylonians. The city of Jerusalem and its temple were destroyed, while the people were carried off to Babylon.

The prophet Ezekiel knew the invasion was coming. As the people of Judah continued sinning, God revealed to Ezekiel that severe judgment was at hand. He proclaimed to the people what would happen to them, but they ignored him. Finally, the inevitable invasion occurred. Ezekiel submitted to the Babylonians so that he could provide spiritual help to his people. He brought hope to the captives, reminding them of God's promise that someday a group would return to Israel to rebuild.

The book of Daniel portrays the people of God in captivity. Daniel and several other young men are brought into the Babylonian court and forced into a three-year course of instruction. But they never forget their worship of God even after they are granted good positions under the Babylonian king. These young men demonstrate their obedience to God despite their captivity, exhibiting heroism and faith in their walk with the Lord when they are threatened with death for their beliefs.

Esther also risked her life in service to God. She was a beautiful young woman who enchanted the Persian king (Persia succeeded the Babylonian Empire) and became the Persian queen even though she

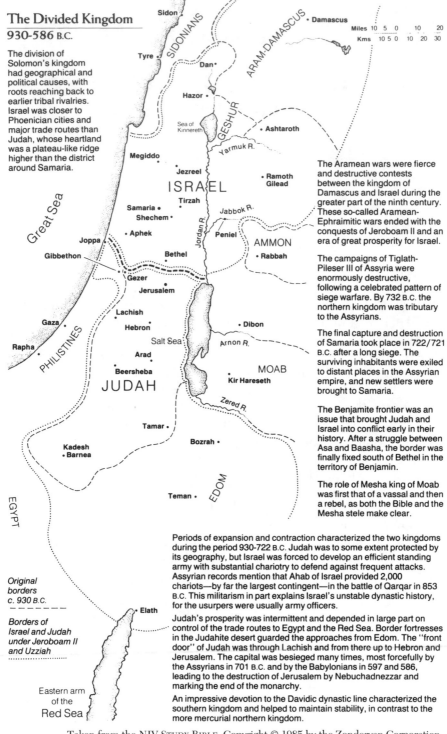

The Divided Kingdom
930-586 B.C.

The division of Solomon's kingdom had geographical and political causes, with roots reaching back to earlier tribal rivalries. Israel was closer to Phoenician cities and major trade routes than Judah, whose heartland was a plateau-like ridge higher than the district around Samaria.

Miles 10 5 0 10 20
Kms 10 5 0 10 20 30

The Aramean wars were fierce and destructive contests between the kingdom of Damascus and Israel during the greater part of the ninth century. These so-called Aramean-Ephraimitic wars ended with the conquests of Jeroboam II and an era of great prosperity for Israel.

The campaigns of Tiglath-Pileser III of Assyria were enormously destructive, following a celebrated pattern of siege warfare. By 732 B.C. the northern kingdom was tributary to the Assyrians.

The final capture and destruction of Samaria took place in 722/721 B.C. after a long siege. The surviving inhabitants were exiled to distant places in the Assyrian empire, and new settlers were brought to Samaria.

The Benjamite frontier was an issue that brought Judah and Israel into conflict early in their history. After a struggle between Asa and Baasha, the border was finally fixed south of Bethel in the territory of Benjamin.

The role of Mesha king of Moab was first that of a vassal and then a rebel, as both the Bible and the Mesha stele make clear.

Periods of expansion and contraction characterized the two kingdoms during the period 930-722 B.C. Judah was to some extent protected by its geography, but Israel was forced to develop an efficient standing army with substantial chariotry to defend against frequent attacks. Assyrian records mention that Ahab of Israel provided 2,000 chariots—by far the largest contingent—in the battle of Qarqar in 853 B.C. This militarism in part explains Israel's unstable dynastic history, for the usurpers were usually army officers.

Judah's prosperity was intermittent and depended in large part on control of the trade routes to Egypt and the Red Sea. Border fortresses in the Judahite desert guarded the approaches from Edom. The "front door" of Judah was through Lachish and from there up to Hebron and Jerusalem. The capital was besieged many times, most forcefully by the Assyrians in 701 B.C. and by the Babylonians in 597 and 586, leading to the destruction of Jerusalem by Nebuchadnezzar and marking the end of the monarchy.

An impressive devotion to the Davidic dynastic line characterized the southern kingdom and helped to maintain stability, in contrast to the more mercurial northern kingdom.

Original borders c. 930 B.C.

Borders of Israel and Judah under Jeroboam II and Uzziah

Eastern arm of the Red Sea

was an Israelite of the tribe of Benjamin. Some of the Persians hated the Israelites and wanted to kill them. Esther defended her people before the king. Because of Esther's heroism, the Israelites were spared certain death. God worked through Esther to protect His people from destruction because through them would arise the Messiah, Jesus Christ.

In this session we will witness one of Ezekiel's attempts to warn God's people about His upcoming judgment. Then we will see how God protected His servant, Daniel, from an evil Babylonian king, bringing judgment through "the writing on the wall." Finally, we will watch God raise Esther to power through the Persian king Xerxes. In all three instances, we will be reminded of God's power in protecting His people.

An Overview

Begin by reading Ezekiel 5. Notice the object lesson which Ezekiel used to communicate God's message of impending judgment. Then read Daniel 5 and see how God worked through one of His people to bring judgment against a wicked Babylonian king. Finally read Esther 2 with the awareness that Esther's rise to power occurred nearly 100 years after the fall of Jerusalem after the Persians had conquered the Babylonian Empire.

The Message in Brief

All three readings stress God's control over historical events. The fall of nations such as Israel and Judah are overseen by God and used for the eventual good of His people. We can be comforted in knowing that even when God's people are carried into exile, God remains with them, protecting them and working through them for His good purposes. God is faithful to His promises. We know that God keeps all of His promises, including His greatest promise—salvation through Jesus Christ.

Working with the Text
A Prophet's "Object Lesson": Ezekiel 5

1. Describe the method by which Ezekiel prophesied the fall of Jerusalem. Whose hair did he use? How did he divide the hair? What was he to do with the various divisions of hair? And what did his actions with each portion of hair represent (v. 12)?

2. What do verses 5–7 suggest are the reasons for God's judgment against Judah?

3. According to Ezekiel 5:10, the siege of Jerusalem would be so severe that the citizens would be forced to employ a cruel method of survival. What would that entail? Now turn to Deuteronomy 28:45–53. How did the Lord predict Jerusalem's fate centuries earlier?

The Writing on the Wall: Daniel 5

1. King Belshazzar's banquet was as a sacrilege against the Lord. In what ways did the king and his nobles invite the judgment of God?

2. How did the Lord communicate His message to the king? What was the king's reaction? Whose advice did the king initially request? Who brought up Daniel's name? And what was Daniel's interpretation of the handwriting?

The Hebrew Queen: Esther 2:1–18

1. Before looking at chapter 2, refer to Esther 1:10–12 and explain why Xerxes' first queen was dethroned. What does this suggest to you about Xerxes' personality?

2. After Queen Vashti was deposed, beautiful girls from all parts of the empire were brought before the king. Describe the beauty treatments these women were given.

3. According to verse 10, Esther, upon her cousin Mordecai's advice, did not reveal her family background and nationality. After reading Esther 3:8–9, explain why this was important. How did Esther deliver her people from certain doom in 7:1–4?

Applying the Message

1. The prophet Ezekiel is known for his strange and provocative "object lessons." Look at the following passages and describe the acts performed by the prophet to communicate his message:

a. Ezekiel 4:1–3

b. Ezekiel 12:3–6

c. Ezekiel 21:6–7

2. Can you share memory of an "object lesson" used in a sermon or children's sermon? Summarize the lesson. Why was it effective in communicating its message?

3. King Belshazzar desecrated and blasphemed the Lord by engaging in pagan worship using vessels taken from the temple in Jerusalem. While using them, he praised the false gods of gold, silver, bronze, iron, wood, and stone. In what ways do you think people desecrate those things which point us to God (e.g., the "cross," the Lord's Supper, God's name, the day of worship, God's Word)?

4. What does the expression "I can see the writing on the wall" mean to you? Discuss how the expression had its origin in the story of Daniel and King Belshazzar.

5. How might Esther, the heroine, be considered a "type" of Jesus Christ? In other words, how does her work in delivering God's people from destruction resemble the work of Jesus Christ?

Taking the Message Home

Review

As time allows, read the entire book of Esther and ponder this remarkable story of beauty, love, courage, and compassion. Look up *Purim* in a dictionary or encyclopedia and consider how Jews continue to celebrate Esther's accomplishment to this day. Reflect on Ezekiel's bizarre methods of prophesying through object lessons. Does God always speak to us in ways that appear "civilized" and full of common sense? Why must we dispense with "reason" and "common sense" when trusting in Jesus' resurrection from the dead? Of what does Job 11:7–8 remind us concerning the ways of God?

Looking Ahead

For a preview of the next session read Nehemiah 1. Consider Nehemiah's feelings when he learned of Jerusalem's condition. Then turn to Zechariah 1:1–6. Had God's people learned their lesson? Had the Lord abandoned them, or does He continue to lead them?

Working Ahead

1. Suppose you were drafted into the military and during a battle you were taken captive. When the war was over you were released from prison and allowed to return home. When you reached home, you discovered everything is gone. There is no more church. Your home is gone as are many of your friends and relatives. What would you do?

2. Spend a little time reflecting on a moment when you felt abandoned by God. How did it feel? Explain what led you to realize God was still with you. Looking back, how can you find comfort in knowing that God was present all along?

3. Church buildings cost a lot of money. It takes the financial support and cooperation of many people to accomplish the construction of a church building. In what ways could the excitement of building a church resemble the excitement felt by God's people as they returned to Israel and rebuilt both their city and temple?

Did you know that until 1853 no mention was found of King Belshazzar in Babylonian records? Nabonidus was known to have been the last king of Babylon. The critics believed this showed the book of Daniel to be fictitious. But in 1853 an inscription was found in a cornerstone of a temple built by Nabonidus in Ur to a god. This inscription read: "May I, Nabonidus, king of Babylon, not sin against thee. And may reverence for thee dwell in the heart of Belshazzar, my firstborn, favorite son." Since then, other inscriptions have shown that Nabonidus was in retirement much of the time outside of Babylon. That meant his son, Belshazzar, was in control of the army and the government and could call himself "king," even though final authority rested with his father. This also explains why Belshazzar made Daniel "the third-highest ruler in the kingdom" (Daniel 5:30). Notice how archaeology can help solve some of the Bible's mysteries!

Session 10

The Rebuilding of a Nation

Ezra 4; Nehemiah 1–2:9; Haggai 2:1–9; Zechariah 8

Approaching This Study

As the prophet Jeremiah foretold, the exile of God's people from Judah lasted nearly 70 years (Jeremiah 25:8–14). These 70 years began with the first deportation of some of the people of Judah in 605 B.C. It concluded with the pronouncement by Cyrus, king of Persia, in 538 B.C. that God's people could return home and rebuild. Not all the exiles returned to Jerusalem. Some had died in captivity; others felt it was better to remain in the foreign land where they had settled. With those exiles who returned to Jerusalem there existed a strong belief that the Messiah would arise from among them. They held fast to their messianic hopes, and they were willing to return to their homeland to rebuild their city in the hope of His coming.

The book of Ezra records Cyrus' decree of liberation for God's people. They could return and rebuild their city and temple. Now Cyrus was not a convert to Judaism. He was simply an enlightened leader who attempted to placate the gods of those he ruled instead of carrying off their images as had been the custom of the Assyrians and Babylonians. In this way, God used Cyrus to fulfill prophecy. According to Ezra, a man named Zerubbabel led the first return to rebuild the temple, guiding 50,000 Israelites back to their homeland. They completed the foundation some two years later, but their success aroused the Samaritans (descendants of those who had once occupied the Northern Kingdom) who opposed further construction and managed to halt work until 522 B.C.

Haggai and Zechariah began preaching some two years later. Haggai worked to ignite enthusiasm among the exiles to renew their building projects. As a result, they were able to finish the temple in 516 B.C. Afterwards, some of the people were discouraged because it wasn't as beautiful as Solomon's temple, but Haggai stressed that the glory of God was far superior than the beauty of any building.

Zerubbabel's Temple

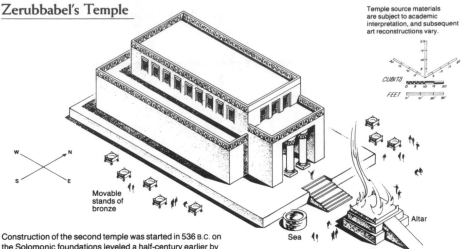

Temple source materials are subject to academic interpretation, and subsequent art reconstructions vary.

CUBITS

FEET

W

N

S

E

Movable stands of bronze

Sea

Altar

Construction of the second temple was started in 536 B.C. on the Solomonic foundations leveled a half-century earlier by the Babylonians. People who remembered the richness of the earlier temple wept at the comparison (Ezr 3:12). Not until 516 B.C., the 6th year of the Persian emperor Darius I (522-486), was the temple finally completed at the urging of Haggai and Zechariah (Ezr 6:13-15).

Archaeological evidence confirms that the Persian period in Palestine was a comparatively impoverished one in terms of material culture. Later Aramaic documents from Elephantine in Upper Egypt illustrate the official process of gaining permission to construct a Jewish place of worship, and the opposition engendered by the presence of various foes during this period.

Of the temple and its construction, little is known. Among the few contemporary buildings, the Persian palace at Lachish and the Tobiad monument at Iraq el-Amir may be compared in terms of technique.

Unlike the more famous structures razed in 586 B.C. and A.D. 70, the temple begun by Zerubbabel suffered no major hostile destruction, but was gradually repaired and reconstructed over a long period. Eventually it was replaced entirely by Herod's magnificent edifice.

© Hugh Claycombe 1986

Chronology: Ezra-Nehemiah

Dates below are given according to a Nisan-to-Nisan Jewish calendar (see chart on "Hebrew Calendar," p. 102).

Roman numerals represent months; Arabic numerals represent days.

540 B.C.

530

520

510

500

490

	YEAR	MONTH	DAY	EVENT	REFERENCE
	539 B.C.	Oct.	12	Capture of Babylon	Da 5:30
	538	Mar.	24	Cyrus's first year	Ezr 1:1-4
	537	to Mar.	11		
	537(?)			Return under Sheshbazzar	Ezr 1:11
	537	VII		Building of altar	Ezr 3:1
	536	II		Work on temple begun	Ezr 3:8
	536-530			Opposition during Cyrus's reign	Ezr 4:1-5
	530-520			Work on temple ceased	Ezr 4:24
	520	VI =Sept.	24 21	Work on temple renewed under Darius	Ezr 5:2; Hag 1:14
	516	XII =Mar.	3 12	Temple completed	Ezr 6:15

Zechariah, who preached at the same time as Haggai, also hoped to inspire completion of the temple. He reminded the people that a right relationship with the Lord was more important than anything else. He, like Haggai, eagerly looked forward to the arrival of the Messiah and the future kingdom He would lead.

Ezra led the second group of exiles back home some 60 years after Zerubbabel's return. He was accompanied by some 5,000 souls in all, divided into 12 family clans. Ezra was determined to restore strict religious observance and revive the national identity of God's people.

Nehemiah led the third return to Jerusalem. Through his leadership, the walls of Jerusalem were rebuilt in 52 days. Nehemiah had been a cupbearer to the king of Persia. But he surrendered his high position to lead God's people and help them renew their covenant with God. Nehemiah's return occurred some 13 years after Ezra's.

Because many among God's people trusted in His promise of a future Messiah, they felt an urgency to return and rebuild Jerusalem and its temple. They believed the existence of such structures marked the ongoing presence of God's grace and providence. When the Messiah, Jesus, arrived, He would demonstrate that God no longer resided in stone and brick structures. The presence of God existed fully in the person and work of Jesus Christ.

	YEAR	MONTH	DAY	EVENT	REFERENCE
	458	I =Apr.	1 8	Ezra departs from Babylon	Ezr 7:6-9
480		V =Aug.	1 4	Ezra arrives in Jerusalem	Ezr 7:8-9
		IX =Dec.	20 19	People assemble	Ezr 10:9
470		X =Dec.	1 29	Committee begins investigation	Ezr 10:16
	457	I =Mar.	1 27	Committee ends investigation	Ezr 10:17
460	445 444	Apr. to Apr.	13 2	20th year of Artaxerxes I	Ne 1:1
	445	I =Mar.-Apr.		Nehemiah approaches king	Ne 2:1
		Aug.(?)		Nehemiah arrives in Jerusalem	Ne 2:11
450		VI =Oct.	25 2	Completion of wall	Ne 6:15
		VII =Oct. to Nov.	8 5	Public assembly	Ne 7:73-8:1
440		VII =Oct.	15-22 22-28	Feast of Tabernacles	Ne 8:14
		VII =Oct.	24 30	Fast	Ne 9:1
430 B.C.	433 432	Apr. to Apr.	1 19	32nd year of Artaxerxes; Nehemiah's recall and return	Ne 5:14; 13:6

Taken from the NIV STUDY BIBLE. Copyright © 1985 by the Zondervan Corporation. Used by permission of Zondervan Publishing House.

An Overview

Read Ezra 4; Haggai 2:1–9; Zechariah 8; and Nehemiah 1–2:9. This will provide a chronological order to the four readings beginning with Zerubbabel's attempt to rebuild the temple, continuing with the exhortations of Haggai and Zechariah to complete the temple, and ending with Nehemiah's departure to rebuild Jerusalem's city walls.

The Message in Brief

Throughout the history of God's people, God has promised to be present in certain places. He was present with Adam and Eve in Eden. He promised to be present among the wandering Israelites in the tabernacle. When the temple was finally built by Solomon, God was considered specially present in the Holy of Holies (the inner sanctuary, where rested the ark of the covenant, which in turn housed the Ten Commandments; no one could enter the Holy of Holies except for the High Priest, and this could only happen once a year). Then Jesus came to earth and demonstrated He was God—the Word made flesh who dwelt among us. And when Jesus ascended, He promised to be specially present among His people in Word and Sacrament. To those returning from exile, then, it was of utmost urgency to rebuild the house of the Lord to assure themselves of God's ongoing presence and grace and to serve as a focal point for the lives of God's people.

Working with the Text

The Building of the Temple Meets Opposition (Ezra 4)

1. After the fall of the Northern Kingdom in 721 B.C., the Assyrian kings exiled the residents of Israel and replaced them with people from other regions of the empire. These individuals worshiped their pagan gods and intermarried with the Israelites who remained. They also practiced a token worship of God, but only as one of their assortment of gods. Thus, the people of the Northern Kingdom, now called "Samaritans," were no longer considered part of God's true people. But why did they want to help Zerubbabel rebuild the temple? What was Zerubbabel's response? Why?

2. By verse 6, the narrator moves to the reign of Xerxes (486–65 B.C.) and in verse 7 the story jumps ahead to the reign of Artaxerxes (465–24 B.C.). These historical leaps are meant to demonstrate Samaria's ongoing attempts to sabotage the rebuilding of Jerusalem. What did the Samaritan letter to Artaxerxes suggest about the disposition of the Jews? Were they depicted as a peace-loving, gentle people? Or were they considered "rabble rousers"? What did the Samaritans suggest the people of Jerusalem would do once they were safely behind the walls of their rebuilt city? Finally, in verse 24, the narrator returns to the rebuilding of the temple under Cyrus, king of Persia around 530 B.C. What happened to the building of the temple? When would work continue?

God's Exhortation to Rebuild (Haggai 2:1–9)

1. In 520 B.C. God tells Haggai to speak His words to Zerubbabel, the governor of Judah. What was God's command? The work on the temple had ceased for several years. According to verse 5, what was the significance of finishing the temple?

2. What does the Lord promise to do with this temple? Whose glory will fill it? And who will come to worship God? Now turn back to Isaiah 60:4–9. In what ways does Isaiah's prophecy echo that of Haggai 2:6–9? Skip to Matthew's account of the Wise Men visiting Jesus in Matthew 2:1–12. Do you see how Haggai's prophecy echoes Isaiah, who in turn foretells the coming of the kings of the east to worship the infant Jesus? So, in a way, the prophecy from Haggai is "messianic" too. It foretells the coming of Jesus Christ. Jesus is "the desired of all nations" mentioned in Haggai 2:7.

God's Presence Returns to Jerusalem (Zechariah 8)

1. How does Zechariah describe life in Jerusalem when God returns to dwell among His people?

2. How does verse 8 indicate that the covenant between God and His people continues after the return from exile?

3. How are God's people to demonstrate their love for Him according to verses 16–19?

Nehemiah Returns to Jerusalem (Nehemiah 1–2:9)

1. Nehemiah's narrative begins in what we would call the months of November and December, 446 B.C. The temple in Jerusalem had been rebuilt, but what was the state of the city walls? Why do you think it was so awful to live in a city without walls?

2. Our text tells us Nehemiah was Artaxerxes' cupbearer. The cupbearer's duties involved choosing the king's wines and tasting them to make sure they weren't poisoned. So King Artaxerxes must have deeply

trusted Nehemiah. When Nehemiah approached the king with great sadness, how did the king demonstrate his concern? What did Nehemiah do before asking the king's favor? What was the king's response to Nehemiah's request?

Applying the Message

1. This session's readings dealt with the rebuilding of Jerusalem and the temple. God gave His people the opportunity to return to their homeland and begin again. Despite the opposition of enemies from Samaria, lethargy, and discouragement, the people rebuilt. What can we learn from these books about building our personal lives with God's help?

2. God used a pagan—Cyrus of Persia—to be His instrument for fulfilling prophecy. Cyrus, having taken over the Babylonian Empire, granted God's people the freedom to return from exile.

How might God use unbelievers to accomplish His good purposes? Give some examples.

3. The people of Judah were determined to rebuild God's house. They believed God's presence would be assured if His house was established. But isn't the glory of God greater than the beauty of any building? Couldn't God be worshiped anywhere? They why do you think it is important for people today to build houses of worship?

4. The rebuilding of the temple helped prepare God's people for the coming of the Messiah, Jesus Christ who would live, die, and rise again to pay for the sins of the world. Believers in Christ know Jesus will again return and judge the world. Why can Christians look forward to the second coming of Christ? How can and does His inevitable return influence our lives?

Taking the Message Home

Review

In reviewing this week's session it would be helpful to read the entire books of Ezra and Nehemiah. Both are relatively short books, and they contain many listings of the individuals involved in the return to Judah and the rebuilding of Jerusalem. These names need not be studied closely. Rather, focus on the narrative of the story.

Looking Ahead

Read the book of Jonah and contemplate the remarkable power of God's will. Truly, one of Jonah's morals is this: You can run but you can't hide! Nevertheless we are given a number of examples of God's grace and forgiveness, and His desire to lead people into greater faith rather than bring instant doom. Reflect on God's great compassion toward the peoples of the world.

Working Ahead

Complete one or more of the following before the next session:

1. Quickly scan Obadiah, Jonah, Nahum, Habakkuk, and Malachi. Which of these books are the longest? Which is the shortest? Which book is the last in the Old Testament?

2. Ask your pastor what it is like to be God's spokesman. Which areas of ministry does he enjoy the most? Which areas are most difficult for him? Ask him whether he would become a pastor again if he could do it all over. Why or why not?

3. Reflect on the last time you prayed to the Lord for help in a difficult situation and He seemed silent. How did you feel? Do you think God was listening? If the problem has since been resolved, be prepared to share with other participants the way in which God was at work?

Did you know that the prophet Zechariah fore- saw a time when the Savior of the world would come to the city of Jerusalem bringing salvation? Interestingly, he would arrive at the city riding on a donkey.

Zechariah 9:9 reads: "Rejoice greatly, O Daughter of Zion! Shout, Daughter of Jerusalem! See, your king comes to you, righteous and having salvation, gentle and riding on a donkey, on a colt, the foal of a donkey." This prophecy was fulfilled one week before Jesus' death when He road into Jerusalem on a donkey while the residents of the nearby communities praised His name. To learn about this story for yourself, read Matthew 21:1–11.

Session 11

Little Known Prophets Who Spoke Great Words

Jonah 1–4; Habakkuk 1:1–4; 3:16–18; Malachi 3:6–4:6

Approaching This Study

The Bible doesn't inform its readers about all the prophets who spoke God's Word in the Old Testament, but it does tell us quite a bit about some of them, and it shares a little about others. We have very little knowledge about Obadiah, Jonah, Nahum, Habakkuk, and Malachi, but we know their ministries were important. Take Obadiah, for example. The name *Obadiah* means "servant of God" or "worshiper of God." His book is only 21 verses long and simply predicts the coming doom of a neighboring nation to Judah called Edom. Nevertheless, it assures God's people of His continuing grace, foreseeing the coming of God's kingdom in Jesus Christ. Because Obadiah was a very common name and there is so little detail in his book, it is difficult to date the time of its writing. But many believe it was written sometime during the Babylonian attacks on Jerusalem. That would make Obadiah a contemporary with Jeremiah.

Or consider Nahum. The name *Nahum* means "comfort," but nothing else is known about the prophet except his hometown (Elkosh) and no one is certain where that is located. Nahum's message attempts to console the people of Judah who live in fear of the Assyrians. It predicts the coming destruction of Assyria's capital, Nineveh, and the promise that God's grace will protect Judah. This probably makes Nahum a contemporary of Zephaniah and a young Jeremiah.

The name *Habakkuk* means "one who embraces." The book of Habakkuk is unique because it consists of a dialog between God and the prophet. Habakkuk protests God's unsearchable ways, questioning the wickedness, turmoil, and oppression which seem so prevalent in Judah. Strangely, God seems to do nothing about such wickedness. But the Lord tells the prophet He will soon bring judgment through the Baby-

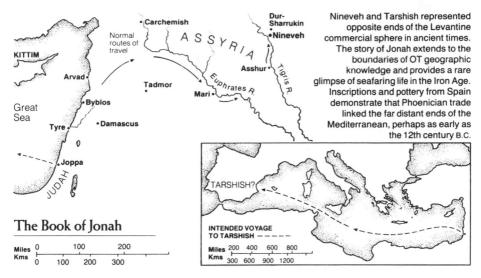

lonians. Habakkuk then wonders how a nation more wicked than Judah could be used as God's instrument of judgment. God makes it clear that the destroyer will eventually be destroyed. So Habakkuk learns to trust in God's plan and power. Habakkuk was probably also a prophet during Jeremiah's time.

Malachi means "my messenger." Malachi was the last prophet of the Old Testament period. There would not be another prophet until John the Baptist, some 400 years later (whose arrival Malachi foresees). The book of Malachi was probably written after Nehemiah had rebuilt the walls of Jerusalem and had returned to Persia. With Nehemiah's absence the people of Israel had again fallen into sin. Nehemiah returned to discover that they were ignoring their tithes and offerings to the Lord, neglecting the Sabbath, and marrying foreign wives. The priests of Judah had become corrupt once again. Because several of these sins are condemned by Malachi, it is likely he wrote sometime after Nehemiah's return to Persia in 433 B.C.

Of the five "minor prophets" considered in this session, Jonah is the most well-known. His name means "dove" and he lived between 800 and 750 B.C. during the reign of Jeroboam II of Israel. We know that because his name is mentioned in 2 Kings 14:25. Jonah, then, was a contemporary of the prophet Amos. Both prophets ministered when Israel and Judah were enjoying great prosperity and political power, but it had succumbed to idolatry and extravagant indulgence. Soon God would bring about the end of the Northern Kingdom through the Assyrian invasion.

Interestingly, as the Assyrian empire expands and begins to threaten its many neighbors, Jonah is sent to the Assyrian capital of Nineveh to demand repentance. Through Jonah, God causes the Ninevites to repent of their sins, sparing them of God's judgment. Thus, the book of Jonah becomes an historical example of God's grace and compassion to all the peoples of the world, not only the people of Israel.

Let's take a look at these final "minor prophets" and grow in our appreciation of their difficult work as God's spokesmen.

An Overview

We will only read passages from three of the five prophets. The readings from Habakkuk and Malachi are about a chapter in length, but they give us a sense of the prophets' concerns and pronouncements. The book of Jonah will be read in its entirety.

The Message in Brief

These three "minor prophets" wrote during different periods of history. Jonah's account occurred some 150 years before Habakkuk's prophecy. And Malachi ministered some 200 years after Habakkuk. Though the prophets lived in different generations amid different political situations, their message is consistent and ongoing. God's people stray, but God remains faithful to His promises and reaches out to His people in grace.

Working with the Text
Jonah and the Big Fish (Jonah 1–4)

1. When Jonah was called by God to preach repentance to Nineveh, what was his reaction? Did God let him flee? Describe how God made sure Jonah fulfilled his mission.

2. When the people of Nineveh repented, God forgave them and did not execute judgment against them. How did Jonah feel about God's

decision? Why? How did the Lord give Jonah an "object lesson" about His compassion for all the peoples of the world?

3. How long was Jonah in the fish? Now look up Matthew 12:39–41 and explain how Jesus used Jonah's experience to foreshadow His own death and resurrection for the sins of the world. Does Jesus view the story of Jonah as a parable or an historical event? How does the mention of Jonah in 2 Kings 14:25 support Jesus' view?

Habakkuk's Faithfulness (Habakkuk 1:1–4; 3:16–18)

1. What is Habakkuk's complaint toward the Lord? Describe the offensive conditions he sees all around him.

2. Habakkuk is reminded of God's wondrous deeds toward the people of Israel throughout history. After recalling God's great acts, Habakkuk is physically weak with awe. How does Habakkuk describe his condition?

3. At the end of Habakkuk's book, the prophet has come to a conclusion about his relationship with God. What will Habakkuk's attitude be toward God despite conditions around him?

Malachi's Warning (Malachi 3:6–4:6)

1. How are God's people "stealing" from the Lord? What is God's promise to the people if they change their ways? What is God's answer to those who question why they should obey the Lord when it seems those who disobey Him prosper?

2. How does Malachi describe the "day of the Lord" for believers in Malachi 4:2? Turn to Luke 1:76–79 and explain how the coming of Jesus is described in a similar fashion.

3. Whom does God promise He will send before the "great and dreadful day of the Lord"? Now look up Matthew 11:11–14 and explain how Malachi's prophecy was fulfilled. What does this suggest about "the day of the Lord"? When did it come and with whom?

Applying the Message

1. After reading passages from these three prophets, do you think it was easy being a prophet? There are those who think preaching and teaching God's Word is rather glamorous, and that it is easier work than many other professions. In what ways do Jonah, Habakkuk, and Malachi indicate that being a spokesman for God can be very difficult work?

2. Jonah tried to run from the Lord, but wherever he went, God followed. Finally, Jonah realized he had no choice but to fulfill God's mission. How can God's inescapable will be of comfort to you, particularly after reading Ephesians 1:11?

3. After reading God's warning and promise about offerings and tithes in Malachi 3:8–12, how might your perspective on "giving" change? When we offer ourselves to God, His church, and others, what will be His response? Do you think His outpouring of blessings will always be material? In what ways might God bless us aside from financial and material gain?

4. Many people today are on the verge of despair over the injustices and inequalities of the world. They lament a nation overwhelmed by crime and violence, and they are saddened by a world so mired in poverty and want. How can Habakkuk's conclusion help us in today's world? See Habakkuk 3:17–18.

5. Sometimes people turn to the Lord late in life. They may have engaged in faithless and wicked acts, hurting themselves and others. Is it a danger to feel outrage against those who turn to the Lord after having led such lives? What does Jesus' love for us motivate us to have for those who turn from the error of their ways and follow the Lord?

Taking the Message Home

Review

Because passages from Nahum and Obadiah were not studied in this session, read these two books in their entirety, noticing when God speaks words of judgment and when He speaks words of grace.

Looking Ahead

Read Ecclesiastes 1:1–11 and think about the writer's attitude. Does he sound depressed to you? Weary? Old? Have you ever viewed the world in such a fashion? How might a person's faith in the Lord help during such periods?

Working Ahead

Complete one or more of the following before the next session:

1. After reading Song of Songs 1, contemplate why this book is found in the Bible.

2. Do you have any favorite expression, maxim, or motto such as "he who laughs last, laughs best", or "God never promises a smooth voyage, only a safe landing"? Be ready to share your favorites during the next session.

3. One of the most famous Psalms is Psalm 23. Memorize this Psalm and spend some time meditating about its meaning for your life.

Did you know that the prophet Nahum predicted the end of Nineveh? Within 20 years after Nahum's prediction the city was besieged by the Babylonians and Medes. After two years of siege a sudden rise of the river washed away part of the walls. Nahum predicted that "the river gates [would be] thrown open" for the destroying army (Nahum 2:6). Through the breach the Babylonians and Medes swept in and utterly destroyed the city. It all came to pass exactly as Nahum had pictured it.

Session 12

The Books of Poetry

Job 1; Psalm 27; Proverbs 4:1–9; Ecclesiastes 1:1–11; Song of Songs 1

Approaching This Study

Some people like poetry; others don't. Some consider poetry too flowery or too difficult to understand. Others see poetry as an effective means for sharing one's feelings.

This session's books are filled with poetry. But the poetry in each book is meant to convey a different message. The book of Job, for example, reflects the cause of suffering. After enduring tremendous catastrophes, Job speaks with his four friends about the reason for his great pain. Does suffering arise from God or Satan, other people or fate? At the end of the book, God Himself intervenes to tell Job all he needs to know.

The book of Psalms is composed of hymns. Many of them were written by King David, who was an accomplished musician. The book of Psalms was used as a hymnal by the people of Judah after their return from captivity and the rebuilding of the temple. It has become known as the "devotional book of the whole world" because its words of prayer and praise are still universally used in worship and private devotion. A number of the Psalms look forward to the coming of the Messiah, Jesus Christ. One of the special features of the Psalms is "parallelism." One kind of parallelism repeats in the second half of the verse what was stated in the first half, but with different words. Another type of parallelism, the second part of the verse contrasts the first part.

In 1 Kings 4:32 we learn that King Solomon spoke 3,000 proverbs! Many of these proverbs, accompanied by those of several other individuals, are incorporated in the book of Proverbs. These maxims largely deal with practical approaches to leading a God-pleasing life. They are written as if a father were teaching his son the ways of the world.

Ecclesiastes was also written by King Solomon. Remember, Solomon was considered the wisest man who ever lived, and one of the richest. His poetry contemplates the source of happiness. With all his wealth, fame, and power, he realizes true happiness can only be found in God. Otherwise, everything in life is meaningless.

Love songs aren't new. We hear them sung all the time. We read them in poetry. The Song of Songs is a long love poem. Its passages express the feelings of love that can exist between a man and a woman. The Song of Songs acts as a meaningful metaphor of the relationship between Christ and His church.

All five books of poetry help the reader in his or her daily walk with the Lord. They express various aspects of our relationship with God, offer practical advice for Christian living, strengthen us through periods of suffering and grief, and direct us to that which is most meaningful in life. Many of the Old Testament books define the history of God's people. Many record the predictions of God's chosen prophets. These five express the feelings that accompany our earthly journey with the Lord. As such, they offer spiritual knowledge and wisdom.

An Overview

Assign different roles for volunteers to read from Job 1. Ask one volunteer to be the narrator, one the voice of Satan, and one the voice of God. Four others could be the voices of the messengers, and one volunteer could read Job's anguished words of worship at the end of the chapter. Then have one person read Psalm 27. Everyone can read Proverbs 4:1–9 together, noticing how advice is given from a father to his son. Ecclesiastes 1:1–11 may be read by a single volunteer. When the first chapter of Song of Songs is read, ask a husband and wife to read, assigning the role of "Beloved" (from the New International Version of the Bible) to the wife, and "Lover" to the husband. All participants can read the section marked "Friends."

The Message in Brief

Some people claim that Christianity brings complete peace and satisfaction. The authors of these five books of poetry indicate that believers also suffer from doubt, pain, depressed feelings, and fear. But such feelings are accompanied by the inevitable certainty that God continues to care and lead, and that in "all things God works for the good of those who love Him, who have been called according to His purpose" (Romans 8:28).

Working with the Text

Why Suffer? (Job 1)

1. The name Satan literally means "accuser." Of what does Satan accuse Job in verses 9–11? In what way is Job afflicted? But what limits does God place on those afflictions?

2. Job had no idea why he suffered so deeply. The reader knows Job had done nothing that deserved such suffering; he understands Job's suffering was a test brought about by Satan's accusation against Job's faith. Although Job never really discovered why he had to endure so much, what do his words in Job 42:1–3 suggest about his attitude toward suffering and God's will?

An Ancient Hymnbook (Psalm 27)

When David wrote this Psalm, how was he feeling? Why? What does David say he would enjoy doing more than anything else?

Practical Advice (Proverbs 4:1–9)

What is the most important acquisition the son can gain according to his father? How is this acquisition personified, that is, given human attributes? Now turn to Proverbs 15:1 and discuss the truth of this maxim.

What Is the Meaning of Life? (Ecclesiastes 1:1–11)

1. Summarize in your own words the feelings expressed by Solomon as he writes this passage. If possible, give examples which support the truth of his statement: "There is nothing new under the sun."

2. In the end, there is only one way to find purpose in life. According to the rich, famous, wise King Solomon, what is the meaning of life according to Ecclesiastes 12:13? Does this answer satisfy you? Why or why not?

God's Love for His Church (Song of Songs 1)

1. What is the Bible's attitude toward erotic love? Is there a place for it in the Christian's life? In what context?

2. Martin Luther wrote: "The [Song of Songs] is a song of praise, in which Solomon praises God for obedience, as for a gift of God. For where God is not Himself the householder and ruler, there is neither obedience nor peace in any station of life. But where there is obedience and good governing, there God dwells, He kisses and embraces His dear bride with His Word, which is the kiss of His lips." Now see if Scripture supports this interpretation of the Song of Songs. Look up Ephesians 5:22–33 and explain.

Applying the Message

1. When Christians are in the midst of suffering, they sometimes question the Lord's will, even as Job did. They are puzzled about the purpose for such pain. In what way could the story of Job help us through the anger and injustice we may feel at such times?

2. The word Satan means "accuser." The term devil means "slanderer." This "slanderer" certainly accused Job. Can you remember moments when Satan and the devil "slandered" and "accused" you through your conscience? How did it make you feel? Of what benefit would the knowledge of Christ's death and resurrection be at such times?

3. In the same way that Israel used Psalms as a hymnbook, almost every church uses a book of hymns to praise God. What are your favorite hymns? Why?

4. Many people believe the maxim "God helps those who help themselves" is found in the book of Proverbs. It is not. As a matter of fact, it is found nowhere in Scripture. After learning about God's grace, why do you think such a statement contradicts the message of Scripture?

5. Solomon's wise words in Ecclesiastes remind us that God's good purposes are at work in the world and that our role is to receive God's

will. This includes making the best of the gifts God has given and accepting the limitations He has placed on us. We are to enjoy life as God grants it and not frustrate ourselves with unrealistic expectations. Above all, we are to demonstrate our faith in Him through obedience to His commandments. In what ways do you think your life could be happier and more fulfilling if you were to follow this lesson?

Taking the Message Home

Review

Page through the book of Psalms. Linger on those that interest you. Start choosing some of your favorites, and don't be hesitant to memorize some!

Looking Ahead

Choose the Old Testament book that is most interesting to you. Read it. List those aspects that seem particularly relevant to you and evaluate why.

Working Ahead

Ask those in your group whether they would enjoy studying one of the Old Testament books at length. Decide which book is most popular and establish a time and place to study together. Use one of the *God's Word for Today* Bible studies available from Concordia Publishing House to guide your study.

Did you know that Psalm 119 is the longest chapter in the Bible? It contains 176 verses divided into 22 sections, each section is headed by a successive letter in the Hebrew alphabet. It is an acrostic poem, which means each stanza within the individual section begins with the same letter of the Hebrew alphabet!

Glossary

adultery. In the Old Testament adultery refers to sexual intercourse between a man and another man's wife. Jesus interprets the Sixth Commandment as forbidding all kinds of sexual indecency in both deed and thought.

amen. The word *amen* is spoken when one wants to express "so be it." It indicates confirmation or agreement.

angels. Literally "messengers." Unseen, spiritual, holy, heavenly beings who continually do God's bidding. Angels protect and serve those who fear God. They differ in rank and dignity.

anoint. To apply oil to a person or thing. Sometimes it was simply a part of grooming. After washing or bathing, people anointed themselves. Hosts anointed their guests as an act of courtesy or respect. Anointing was also done at a person's induction to the office of priest or king. Christ was anointed with the Holy Spirit.

Antichrist. One who is both an enemy of Christ and a usurper of His rights and names.

apocalyptic literature. These include the books of Daniel and Revelation, which reveal events of the Last Times, judgment, and the hereafter. Apocalyptic literature uses numbers and symbols to express certain ideas.

Baptism. Christian Baptism must include the application of water in the name of the triune God, Father, Son, and Holy Spirit. The way the water is applied to the individual, however, can vary. The New Testament makes no distinction between adult and infant baptism. Christian baptism works the forgiveness of sins; it delivers one from spiritual death and the devil; it gives eternal salvation to all who believe in Christ; it offers the Holy Spirit. Baptism also makes one a member of the body of Christ, the church.

Christ. Greek for the Hebrew *messiah*, which means "anointed one." Jesus is the promised Messiah.

church. The collected gathering of God's people. The New Testament speaks of the church both as the Christians gathered in a specific place and as all Christians everywhere of all time. It is also described as the fellowship of God's people, the bride of Christ, the body of Christ, and a building of which Jesus Christ is the chief cornerstone.

circumcision. Removal of the foreskin of the penis. God instituted the rite of circumcision upon Abraham and his descendants. It showed that He would be their God, and they were to belong to Him. The Hebrew people looked down on those who were not circumcised. Controversy erupted in the early Christian church between Jewish Christians who demanded that Gentiles be circumcised in order to be Christian and the Gentiles who refused. St. Paul spoke God's Word to this controversy when he declared that circumcision was not required of Gentiles who became Christians.

congregation. An assembly of people.

conversion. An act of God's grace by which a sinful person is turned around and brought into God's kingdom. Conversion is accomplished by the Holy Spirit, who brings the person to faith in Christ through the Word.

covenant. An agreement between two or more tribes, nations, or individuals to do or refrain from doing something.

deacon. Someone who serves. In the early church deacons were chosen to relieve the apostles of caring for the physical needs of widows and other poor people.

demons. Evil spirits who are against God and His work. They are angels who rebelled against God and now follow Satan.

doctrine. Something that is taught; instruction or teaching.

Easter. Teutonic goddess of light and spring. By the eighth century the name was applied to Christ's resurrection.

elder. In the New Testament *elder* and *bishop* are used to mean the same thing: overseer. The elder or presbyter was a man the apostles appointed in each Christian congregation to be its spiritual leader.

elect. The elect are those who have faith in Christ as the promised Messiah and Savior.

election. The New Testament spells out the doctrine of election. No one deserves to be saved. God, however, desires from eternity that all people be saved. By God's grace through faith alone in Jesus people are saved. Those who have received God's gift of faith respond in thankfulness to God for His love and grace in choosing them.

epistle. A formal letter that includes Christian doctrine and instruction.

eternal life. Eternal life begins when the Holy Spirit by grace brings a person to faith in Jesus Christ. Although the Christian already has eternal life, he or she will not experience it fully until the resurrection of the body and the life of the world to come.

faith. That belief and trust in the promise of God in Christ Jesus, worked by the Holy Spirit, through which a person is declared just, brought into a right relationship with God, saved. The Holy Spirit works faith in Christ in the individual through the Gospel and the Word and the Sacraments.

fellowship. The basic idea of fellowship is that of sharing something in common. Christian fellowship shares the common bond of the Gospel, faith in

Christ, and various spiritual gifts. Through the work of the Holy Spirit believers have a oneness in Christ.

forgiveness. God's act whereby He ends the separation caused by peoples' sins and puts them back into a proper relationship with Himself. Forgiveness is a gift of God, given out of grace for Christ's sake. As a result of Christ's forgiveness, we are to forgive our neighbor. Recognizing and being sorry for our sins precedes forgiveness.

gentiles. Non-Hebrew nations of the world. People outside the Jewish faith.

glory. That which shows the greatness of someone or something. The glory of God is shown in and by His great miracles, His eternal perfection, His creation, and all His works. Most important, it is shown by His Son, our Lord Jesus Christ.

Gnosticism. A system of belief that reached its peak in the second and third centuries. According to the Gnostics, salvation came by hating the world and everything physical and by escaping to the spirit world. They said Jesus came not to save people from sin but to show them how to escape to the spiritual world.

Gospel (Good News). The Good News that God has forgiven all people because Jesus Christ has fulfilled the Law in their place and paid the penalty for their sin on the cross.

gospels. The first four books of the New Testament. Matthew, Mark, Luke, and John each wrote one of the books. They are called gospels because they tell the good news of how salvation was won for all people by Jesus Christ.

grace. God's undeserved love and favor in Jesus Christ by which He is moved to forgive people's sins and grant them salvation. The word *grace* is sometimes used as a gift, quality, or virtue. Saving grace, however, is none of these things. It is a quality within God. It is also referred to as God's steadfast love or faithfulness.

heaven. The invisible world or universe from which God rules; the home of angels. Christ rules from heaven and receives believers there. *See also* paradise.

heir. The individual to whom another person's wealth or possessions, the person's inheritance, is given after the person dies.

hell. Either the place of eternal punishment or the punishment itself.

heresy. Stubborn error in an article of faith in opposition to Scripture.

holy. That which is set apart to be used for or by God. Holiness is the state of being without sin. The holiness of God is imparted to people through His act of choosing them in grace and through His other mighty acts. It culminates in the saving work of Jesus Christ.

hymn. A song telling about God and praising Him.

inspiration. The special way the Holy Spirit worked in certain people to cause them to act out, speak, or write God's Word. When the Holy Spirit did this, the person who was inspired was certainly under the direction of God's power (God-breathed), but he or she was not a robot.

Israel. (1) The name given to Jacob after he wrestled with an intruder (Genesis 32:28): (2) The name of the nation composed of the descendants of Jacob and his 12 sons. Jacob and his sons founded the 12 tribes of Israel. (3) The name given to the 10 northern tribes of Israel after Solomon's death, when they revolted under Rehoboam and the kingdom split in two. The Northern Kingdom was called Israel to distinguish it from the Southern Kingdom, which was called Judah. (4) This name is also used to describe all who follow in the faith of Abraham, Isaac, and Jacob and therefore are true Israelites, no matter what their physical descent.

Jesus. Greek for the Hebrew name *Joshua,* which means "savior."

Jew. Originally someone who belonged to the tribe or Kingdom of Judah as opposed to those in the Northern Kingdom. *Hebrew* denotes those who descended from Abraham; *Israel* denotes those who descended from Jacob; and *Jew* denotes those who descended from the tribe or Kingdom of Judah.

Jordan River. The most important river in Palestine. It is the river in which Jesus was baptized by John. The river is 3 to 10 feet deep and about 100 feet wide.

Judah. (1) The fourth son of Jacob and Leah. Jacob bestowed the blessing of the birthright on Judah. Jesus was one of Judah's descendants. (2) The tribe that descended from Judah. It occupied the greater part of southern Palestine. (3) The kingdom of Judah which began when the 10 northern tribes withdrew from Rehoboam around 912 B.C. and lasted until 587 B.C., when Jerusalem fell. It existed in the southern part of Palestine.

justification. The gracious act of God by which He pronounces all people to be not guilty of their sin through faith in Jesus. The basis for His acquittal is that Jesus Christ fulfilled the Law in humanity's place and paid the penalty for all people's sin as He suffered and died on the cross.

kingdom of God. A spiritual kingdom that includes all nations. The New Testament pictures God's kingdom as the Holy Spirit in the hearts of His people. The kingdom of God is, at times, spoken of as a future blessing, as in the kingdom Jesus will bring on the Last Day, and, at times, as a present reality. The church proclaims the kingdom of God by preaching the Gospel.

Lord. (1) LORD (often printed in capital and small capital letters in the Bible) is God's personal name. It comes from the Hebrew word *Yahweh.* (2.) Lord (capital *L* and the remaining letters lowercase) comes from the Hebrew word *adon.* It means "master" and denotes ownership. (3) *Adonai* is the word the Israelites said whenever they saw the consonants of Yahweh

(YHWH). (4) The Greek word *kyrios* is also translated as Lord. It is the word used for a human master or for God as the ruler. It is also the word used for Christ, who by His death and resurrection is Lord.

Lord's Supper. Christ instituted this supper on the night of His betrayal to replace the Passover feast. It is a memorial for His death for the sins of the world. In this meal Christ gives His body and blood together in, with, and under the bread and wine. Christians who trust in the blessings Christ promises to give in this meal and partake of it in faith receive the forgiveness of sins, life, and salvation, and a strengthening of their faith. Also called "Breaking of Bread," "Holy Communion," "Eucharist," and "the Lord's Table."

love. Various types of love are referred to in the Bible. The Greek word *agape* represents God's love for sinful people. This is the kind of love Christians are to have.

mercy. God's undeserved favor and love within the covenant relationship.

Messiah. Hebrew for "the anointed one." *See* Christ.

minister. A person who has been called—by God, through the church—to active service to God. All Christians have vocations—callings by God in life; and all baptized Christians have received various gifts of the Holy Spirit. All Christians are members of the priesthood of all believers (1 Peter 2:9). However, ministers have a distinct calling from God, even as Jesus chose 12 of His disciples to serve as apostles.

miracle. An event that causes wonder; something that takes place outside of the laws of nature. The New Testament depicts miracles as acts of power, signs, and wonders. Their significance could be understood only by those who had faith in Jesus Christ.

ordination. A rite (act) of the church by which the church through a congregation publicly confers the pastoral office on a qualified man. Ordination has its historical roots in the New Testament and in the early church. In the New Testament, deacons, missionaries, and elders were called to their offices, just as today a congregation calls a man to be its pastor.

parable. A method of speech that compares two objects for the purpose of teaching a moral or religious truth. It is an earthly story with a heavenly or spiritual meaning. Although the events and characters in the parable are true to nature, not every detail of the story has a spiritual meaning. Rather there is only one main point of comparison. Jesus often spoke in parables to teach the people about Himself and the kingdom of heaven.

paradise. Used in the New Testament to describe heaven, the home of those who die in Christ.

peace. Often used to describe that state of spiritual tranquility and harmony that God gives when He brings one into a right relationship with Himself.

Pentecost. The Jewish Feast of Weeks, which was celebrated 50 days after the Feast of Passover. It is also known as the Feast of Harvest and the Day of Firstfruits. On this day the Holy Spirit was outpoured on the disciples, and many people came to faith in Christ.

prayer. Speaking with God. Prayers can be formal or spoken freely from one's own thoughts and concerns. They can be said together by a large group of believers or alone by an individual. They can be said at set times and places or all times and places.

priest. One who represents the people before God. Through Moses, God appointed Aaron and his descendants as priests. They wore special clothing in the sanctuary, taught the people, and inquired of God's will. The chief priest, or high priest, was in charge of all the other priests. He offered the sin offering, made sacrifice on the Day of Atonement, and discovered the will of God through Urim and Thummim. In the New Testament, Jesus Christ is the only high priest. Since He sacrificed Himself for the sins of the people and this sacrifice need never be repeated, there is no longer a need for the Levitical priesthood. The New Testament also teaches the priesthood of all believers. Christians share in Christ's priestly activity by bringing the Gospel to people.

Redeemer, redemption. The buying back of humanity from sin and death by Christ, who paid the price with His perfect obedience and His sacrificial death on the cross.

repentance. A total change of heart and life that God works in an individual who does not believe or trust in Him by turning him or her around to one who does believe and trust in Him. Repentance includes both sorrow for one's sins and faith in Christ through whom forgiveness is granted.

resurrection. A return to life after one has died.

righteous. That which is right in accordance with the Law. The term is particularly used to describe people who are in a right relationship with God through faith.

sacrament. A word the church uses to describe a sacred act instituted by God where there are visible means connected to His Word. In a sacrament God offers, gives, and seals to the individual the forgiveness of sins earned by Christ.

sacrifice. An act of worship where a person presents an offering to God. Sacrifices were practiced from ancient times to atone for sins and to express thankfulness to God. Sacrifices were offered for various purposes. Among the main ones mentioned in the Old Testament are the sin offering, the trespass offering, the burnt offering, the peace offering, the meal and drink offerings, and the heifer offering. Offerings were sacrificed on the altar morning and evening, at each Sabbath and new moon, and at the three leading festivals. All sacrifices point to and are fulfilled in Christ, the Lamb of God, sacrificed for the sins of the world.

salvation. Deliverance from any type of evil, both physical and spiritual. Spiritual salvation includes rescue from sin. It is a gift of God's grace through faith in Christ.

Satan. The chief fallen angel and enemy of God, humanity, and all that is good. Sometimes called Abaddon, Apollyon, or Beelzebul.

Son of Man. Jesus used this title to emphasize the power and dominion He receives from the Ancient of Days. (See Daniel 7 and Matthew 16:27.)

Son of God. The title is applied to Jesus in a unique sense. It says that Jesus as the Son is equal to God the Father.

suffering servant. Jesus is the fulfillment of the suffering servant spoken about in the Old Testament (Isaiah 42:1–4, 52:13–53:12).

sin. Sin is both doing what God forbids and failing to do what He commands. Because of sin everyone deserves temporal and eternal death. Only through faith in Christ, who kept God's Law perfectly and suffered the punishment for the sins of the world, does one escape the results of sin.

soul, spirit. The soul is not separate from the body; rather it is that which gives life: it animates the flesh. It is the inner person as distinguished from the flesh. The soul departs at death. It is the seat of the appetites, emotions, and passions. It can be lost and saved.

tabernacle. The movable sanctuary in the form of a tent.

temple. The fixed sanctuary of the Lord.

testament. *See* covenant.

tithe. A tenth part of one's income. According to the Law, a tenth of all produce of land and herds was sacred to the Lord.

transfiguration. The name given to the time when Jesus was visibly glorified in the presence of His three disciples.

trinity. The church's term for the coexistence of Father, Son, and Holy Spirit in the unity of the Godhead; three distinct Persons in one divine Being, or Essence. The term *Trinity* does not occur in the Bible, but many passages support the doctrine of the Trinity.

unleavened. Bread without yeast. The Israelites ate unleavened bread at Passover as a reminder of the Exodus.

will. Inclination or choice. God's will is that which He determines. It is revealed in His acts, His Law, and especially in Christ. Humanity's fallen or natural will cannot will good. God's grace alone is able to incline a person's will to good.

Word. God's Word comes to people in various forms, for example, through speaking, writing, visions, and symbols. Jesus Christ is the supreme revelation of God. He is the living Word.

works. Whether a person's works are good or bad depends on that person's relationship to God. Only a person who believes in Jesus Christ as Savior can do good works in God's eyes, since good works are a fruit of faith.

world. Used not only to describe the universe or the human race, but often to denote the wicked and unregenerate, those who are opposed to God.

worship. To bow down, kiss the hand, to revere, work, serve. The respect and reverence given to God. New Testament worship is centered in and around the Word of God. It involved reading Scripture and psalms, singing hymns and spiritual songs, teaching, praying, and celebrating the Lord's Supper.